So Great a Cloud

So Great a Cloud

A Record of Christian Witness

17/8/0́9

Stephen Redmond SJ

Priest in holiday house
Ballinskelligs

VERITAS

First published 2009 by
Veritas Publications
7/8 Lower Abbey Street
Dublin 1, Ireland
Email publications@veritas.ie
Website www.veritas.ie

ISBN 9781847301253

10 9 8 7 6 5 4 3 2 1

Designed by Barbara Croatto
Printed in the Republic of Ireland by ColourBooks, Dublin.

Veritas books are printed on paper made from the wood pulp of managed
forests. For every tree felled, at least one tree is planted, thereby renewing natural
resources.

'Having therefore so great a cloud of witnesses, let us throw off everything that weighs us down, every clinging sin, let us run with determination the race set before us with our eyes fixed on Jesus, from whom faith comes and in whom faith is crowned.'
Hebrews 12:1-2a

*In grateful tribute to all, beginning with my parents,
who helped me along the way of faith.*

ACKNOWLEDGEMENTS

There is hardly any need for me to write an 'inspirational' foreword. The Hebrews text on the title page says it all. Here I want to say 'thank you' to those who helped to make the book:

To the editors of the magazines (especially of *The Pioneer*) in which much of the material first appeared; to Veritas (especially Catherine Gough for her editing so courteously done and to Vivienne Adu-Boahen for the cover artwork); to the printer and to the Milltown Park library staff.

Writing a book like this entails not only author's formulation ('My words are my own', to quote Charles II of England), particular emphases and (one hopes) some personal insight, but also the ascertaining of facts. In my fact-finding I have been greatly helped by various authors and informants. My thanks to them all. Nearly all these presenters of outstanding Christians, as I may call them, are listed under 'Sources'.

Stephen Redmond SJ
John Austin House
Dublin
2008

CONTENTS

PART II

TWENTIETH-CENTURY TESTIMONY

PART I

From Peter to Thérèse

THE ROCK

PETER

'Andrew first found his brother Simon and said to him, "we have found the Messiah" [which means Christ]. He brought him to Jesus. Jesus looked at him and said, "so you are Simon the son of John? You shall be called Kephas" [which means Rock]'.

So it was, according to the Gospel of John, that Christ and Peter met for the first time. The gospels of Matthew, Mark and Luke show Peter being called to discipleship with his brother Andrew at the Sea of Galilee. It seems that John was recording a preliminary call and the other gospels recorded the definitive one.

John also tells us that Peter, along with Andrew and Philip, came from Bethsaida, 'The House of the Fishermen'. Matthew, Mark and Luke mention Peter and his mother-in-law at Capernaum, another lake-side town. Luke says that he and Andrew fished in partnership with James and John, the sons of Zebedee.

The relationship between Christ and Peter is one of the most amazing features of the gospels. Each is, as it were, a foil to the other, bringing out the other's reality, the other's 'heart'. Quite clearly the gospel-forming Church of the very early years realised that Simon the Rock was a Very Important Person in the Christ-event. He is always named first in lists of the Twelve and appears in one unforgettable scene after another, scenes which, when put together, make a sort of fifth gospel: the Gospel of Peter – Peter searching for Jesus at prayer, in the storm on the lake, protesting to and admonished by Jesus, accepted by Jesus as the spokesman of the Twelve, given a unique stewardship in the Church, first-named of the privileged trio with Jesus on certain occasions and the only individual recorded in the gospels as prayed for by Jesus.

In the Passion the relationship is sheer drama: the feet-washing scene at the Last Supper, 'I will never fall away ... you will deny me'; sleeper and swordsman in Gethsemane; and most dramatic of all, his denials (given in all four gospels – no cover-ups here): 'the Lord turned and looked at Peter' (Luke), 'and he broke down and wept' (Mark).

John provides a graphic picture of him on Easter morning running to the tomb with the beloved disciple and going in and viewing the graveclothes. Luke briefly reports an appearance of the risen Lord to him. He is highlighted in great detail in the last chapter of John: splashing ashore to meet Jesus, attesting his love, being made pastor of the people of God, promised martyrdom and told, as before, to 'follow me'. Even at this ecstatic Easter moment the ever-human Peter is curious to know what will happen to the beloved disciples and is (surely, serenely and gently) told to mind his own business, which is to say 'follow me'.

Some great gospel lines of Peter's are part of the rich Christian heritage of prayer: 'Depart from me for I am a sinful man'; 'Lord, to whom shall we go?'; 'You have the words of eternal life … You are the Holy One of God'; 'You are the Christ, the Son of the living God'; 'Lord, you know everything, you know that I love you.'

In the first half of the Acts of the Apostles, Peter is the leading figure of the infant Church. He initiates the election of Matthias as one of the Twelve, gives the Pentecost proclamation and confronts the religious establishment with the Easter Good News. He gains a reputation as a miracle-worker, is imprisoned and scourged with his colleagues and preaches with John in Samaria. He welcomes the new and alarming convert Paul of Tarsus. 'I remained with Kephas fifteen days,' Paul says in his letter to the Galatians. An intriguing interlude in which, surely, Peter poured out his memories of Jesus, Paul linked these memories with his own revelation of the risen Lord and each became acquainted with the other while they discussed the prospects of the Church.

At Joppa (modern Jaffa), Peter had a spiritual experience comparable to that of Paul on the road to Damascus. It convinced him that Christ was meant for Gentiles as well as for Jews, and it was immediately followed by his reception of the centurion Cornelius and his relatives and close friends into the Church.

Back in Jerusalem, he defended his pro-Gentile stance and was imprisoned by King Herod Agrippa. After his escape he went 'to another place' – this was perhaps Antioch, where an important Christian community was developing. We know on the evidence of Paul that he was in Antioch at some stage, where Paul rebuked him for holding aloof from Gentile Christians out of fear of what Paul called 'the circumcision party'. The rebuke can be read as a recognition of Peter's importance and influence. He was in Jerusalem for the debate regarding whether Gentile converts were bound by the law of Moses, especially with reference to circumcision. Peter strongly and effectively said no, thus helping to liberate the Church for its mission to the nations.

There is a very ancient and very strong tradition that Peter was martyred in Rome during Nero's persecution, 64–68 AD. This tradition is confirmed by early Roman 'Peter-cult' and the fact that no other local church claimed him as its 'own' martyr. Therefore, it can be safely accepted.

And so the Easter promise of John 21 was fulfilled: the old man Peter held out his hands and was bound fast and taken to death. *Saint of companionship with Christ, of mission from Christ, of return to Christ after failure and prayed for by Christ – pray for us.*

> *Hands once good at nets and oars are tied*
> *I think of other hands: nailed, crucified*
> *I saw them at the lake: so different*
> *wounded still but vibrant, radiant*
> *signalling hope and love, outstretched to give*
> *saying, 'Like me you'll die, like me you'll live'.*
> *And so I'll die and come ashore*
> *home at last forevermore*
> *with One who keeps his promises*
> *his hands in mine and mine in his.*

THE LIGHT ON THE ROAD

PAUL

Tarsus in southern Turkey is an ancient city, dating back at least nine centuries before Christ. It became a busy port and a centre of education, part of the Greek culture-zone of the eastern Mediterranean. Extending Roman power eastwards, Pompey – Julius Caesar's rival – made it the capital of the new province of Cilicia. It was at Tarsus that Cleopatra first dazzled Mark Antony; so began the famous and fateful relationship that ended so tragically. Antony gave Tarsians the privilege of Roman citizenship, a status confirmed by the man who defeated him and Cleopatra and became the master of the Roman world: Caesar Augustus.

It was in the reign of Augustus, possibly in the first decade of the Christian era, that the most famous citizen of Tarsus in its long history was born. He was a member of the Jewish community there. His name was Saul. Like many Jews of that period, he also had a Greek or Roman name: Paul. (Names of similar sound were often chosen.)

His double name reflected the double world in which he lived. He was, as he insisted, 'of the people of Israel, of the tribe of Benjamin, a Hebrew born of Hebrews, as to the law [of Moses] a Pharisee.' (Phil 3:5) But his Gentile environment affected him too: we see it in his references to Greek sport, in his attitude to Roman authority, in his taking advantage of his Roman citizenship, in the vibrant Greek of his epistles.

In due course, Saul-Paul went to Jerusalem to study under the famous rabbi Gamaliel (mentioned in the Acts of the Apostles as advising the religious leaders to be cautious in their treatment of Jesus' followers) to become a rabbi himself. Rabbis needed a trade as they were forbidden to make money by their teaching; Saul-Paul took up tent-making.

We do not know whether the tent-maker of Tarsus ever met the carpenter of Nazareth. We do know from his first appearances in the Acts of the Apostles that he regarded the proclamation of Jesus as Messiah and Risen One as an intolerable blasphemy and a major menace to the faith of his people. Luke's first picture of his future hero shows him guarding the clothes of the stoners of Stephen and approving of the killing – the angry young man was on fire against the new creed. Years later he told King Herod Agrippa and the Governor Festus: 'I was convinced that I ought to do many things in opposing the name of Jesus of Nazareth ... In raging fury I persecuted them even to foreign cities.' Luke set out for Damascus on his anti-Jesus crusade, and so to the great U-turn, the most famous conversion in the history of the Church.

We have three accounts in the Acts of the Apostles of this 'moment of truth'. The last of them is in Paul's address to Herod Agrippa and Festus: 'I saw on the way a light from heaven, brighter than the sun ... I heard a voice saying to me in the Hebrew language, "Saul, Saul, why do you persecute me? It hurts you to kick against the goad". And I said, "Who are you, Lord?" And the Lord said "I am Jesus whom you are persecuting"'. This experience of Jesus as Lord and the realisation of the union between Jesus and his people transformed Paul's whole life and thought.

The next decade or so of his life is a tale of four cities: Damascus, where he was baptised and preached his first Christian homilies; Jerusalem, where he met the community he had tried to destroy; his native Tarsus; and Antioch, where he joined a community of both Jews and Gentiles. Barnabas from Cyprus was his stand-by and intermediary in this period, making him acceptable to the Jerusalem believers and bringing him from Tarsus to Antioch where, Luke tells us, 'the disciples were for the first time called Christians'.

This splendid capital of Syria was symbolic of the cosmopolitan world to which Paul was called to preach the gospel. Mission One took him to Barnabas' native Cyprus and to part of what is now southern Turkey. He moved from one synagogue to another in a flux of conversion and opposition. He took part in the 'Council of Jerusalem', helping it to its momentous and Church-liberating decision that Gentile converts should not be subject to Jewish observance, especially circumcision. Thus encouraged, he plunged into Mission Two, which brought him across what is now Turkey into Macedonia and Greece. Names of new communities appear, to which he afterwards wrote epistles: Galatia, Philippi, Thessalonica and, best known of all, Corinth, where he found better gospel ground than in its more sceptical neighbour Athens.

Ephesus, the capital of Asia (the Roman name for much of what is now western Turkey), which housed the great temple of Artemis (Diana), was the centre of Mission Three. His long stay there climaxed in the riot of the silversmiths, who felt that he was damaging their trade in Artemis shrines. Then back to Jerusalem where he ran into more trouble which came in the shape of Asian Jews who incited a riot against him. He was rescued by the Roman commandant who sent him for safety and trial to the governor Felix at Caesarea, who detained him for two years without trial. Felix's successor Festus commenced his trial in Caesarea but suggested transferring it to Jerusalem. But Paul, as a Roman citizen, 'appealed to Caesar'. And so to sea, under military guard.

Chapter 27 of Acts is a classic of 'voyage narrative': Luke at his best, writing as an eye-witness and focusing on Paul as the most important passenger. The voyage ends in shipwreck off Malta. After a stay there it was north to Rome, where Paul begins his house arrest: 'He lived there two whole years at his own expense, welcoming all who came to him, preaching the kingdom of God and teaching about the Lord Jesus Christ quite openly and unhindered'. So ends the Acts. Paul probably went east again and may have gone to Spain. According to reliable tradition in the early church, he died a martyr in Rome in the persecution of Nero, AD 64–68.

His epistles, accepted by all Christians as inspired scripture, are of course a treasury of doctrine – personally, passionately, intuitively expressed. All is centred on Christ: the crucified and risen Lord; Head of his Body the Church; liberator from sin; trail-blazer of his people into glory; and embodiment of a divine love that will ultimately transform the cosmos. Christian living is commitment to Christ. Its heart is love and its special bond is the Eucharist.

The epistles also provide us with precious pieces of autobiography, for example, 2 Corinthians and Galatians. With the Acts of the Apostles they admit to us the Pauline portrait gallery men and women whose lives touched his: fellow-missionaries Barnabas, John Mark, Silas, Timothy and Titus; fellow-tentmaker Aquila and his wife Priscilla; Luke the physician, Claudius the commandant, Julius the centurion, Demetrios the silversmith and Lydia the fabric-dealer; Onesimus the slave and Philemon his master; the jailer of Philippi and the town-clerk of Ephesus, among others.

Paul of Tarsus, and of so many other places, moved in a world which in some ways was very like our own. He presented this world with a challenge and hope: Christ is Lord and his lordship is truly person-to-person and cosmic. It is clear that his heart went out to the communities he founded; points of light in the pagan darkness of the Greco-Roman world, with their faith, we may suppose, flickering from time to time. We may also suppose that in the communion of saints he prays for communities in similar circumstances today.

It is also clear that he was very convinced of God's grace in him. For him God was present and active. In this he is a saint for all of us as we travel along our own roads of life.

I thought I was so right:
defend tradition
stamp out, destroy.
And then a blinding light:
a voice, a mission
new life, new joy.

WOMEN TOGETHER

PERPETUA AND FELICITY

In the ninth century before Christ, voyagers from Tyre in the present Lebanon founded a colony on the North African coast in what is now Tunisia. They called it 'Quart Hadasht' – 'New City', Carthage. It became the centre of a great commercial empire in the western Mediterranean. Across the sea in Italy another power was developing: Rome. Carthage and Rome clashed in three wars spanning more than a century. Even after winning two wars the Romans feared Carthage and provoked their enemies into a third. The end came in 146 BC when the Romans captured the great city after a three-year siege, razed it to the ground and salted the site. The Carthagenian territory became the Roman province of 'Africa'.

In the following century, by favour of Julius Caesar and Augustus, Carthage was re-founded. It became the centre of Roman rule in that part of the empire, and one of the finest cities of the empire with its temples, pro-consul's palace, elegant houses, aqueduct, public baths and amphitheatre. And so on to 'Women Together'.

The first definite picture we have of Christians in Carthage is a martyrdom in July 180 AD. The martyrs came from Scillium (the exact location of which is not known with certainty) but their trial was in Carthage. Their Acts is the oldest extant document of the Church in that part of Africa. About twenty years later the Church in Carthage and other Christian communities faced another persecution when the emperor Septimius Severus forbade conversion to Judaism and Christianity.

Among those arrested were the catechumens Vibia Perpetua, a young wife and mother of upper-class family, and Felicity, a slave girl (probably of Perpetua's household) and Revocatus, Saturninus and Secundulus. They were joined by Saturus, who was probably their catechist.

We have a remarkable account of the 'Carthage Six' in *The Passion of Saints Perpetua and Felicity*. About one half of it is attributed to Perpetua herself and smaller segments to Saturus and an eye witness, perhaps the great Tertullian, who was a leading light of the Carthage community. It was circulated widely in the early Church. It can be considered as 'instant reportage'.

The 'Passio' is very detailed. It described Perpetua's father's attempts to get her to change her mind, her imprisonment, her mystical experiences, her joy at having her baby boy with her, the baptism of the five, the public trial with appeals to renounce the faith from both governor and father and the unspeakable sentence: exposure to the beasts in the amphitheatre as part of the celebration of the Caesar Geta's birthday.

Felicity had her special crisis and expression of faith. She was pregnant and because the law forbade the execution of pregnant women, she feared that her death would be postponed and so she would die with criminals. Her companions prayed and shortly before the amphitheatre day she gave birth to a son. When she was in labour, a guard asked her how she would endure the ravaging of the beasts, she replied: 'Now I suffer what I suffer. Then another will suffer for me because I shall be suffering for Him' – a statement of the mysticism of martyrdom.

And so to the amphitheatre. At Perpetua's insistence the five companions (Secundulus had died in prison) entered the arena in their own dress and not in the dress of pagan ritual. She and Felicity were exposed to a wild heifer: 'Perpetua was tossed first and fell on her back … She got up, saw that Felicity had been knocked down and went over to her, gave her her hand and lifted her up and the two of them stood together.'

In a brief interval, Perpetua exhorted her catechumen brother to 'stand in the faith' and Saturus said to a soldier, 'Let these things strengthen, not disturb you,' soaked the man's finger-loop in his blood and gave it to him as a memento and a pledge.

Then the final scene came: the five sealing their martyrdom with a kiss of peace and accepting the sweep of the dagger, with Saturus dying first and Perpetua, having lamented over the broken bodies, guiding the unsteady hand of the young, inexperienced gladiator to her throat.

Today visitors to Carthage see what has been uncovered of the ancient city. Like Perpetua's father, they climb the hill to the citadel area where the prison was located. They read the names of the 'Carthage Six' on an ancient memorial stone, discovered in 1907. They stand in the arena where two brave women stood together in love unto death for Christ. If they are pilgrims they pray to them and give thanks for them – as we can too.

They stand together, pray and wait
in horror world of pain and hate
and then in glory, swift and free
their Lover comes eternally.

WHEAT AND BREAD

IGNATIUS, POLYCARP, JUSTIN, CALLISTUS AND CYPRIAN

Ignatius

During its first few centuries, the Christian Church was subject to outbursts of horrific persecution by the Roman State; it was an era of martyrs. Here we salute five of the very many who, in the words of one of the five, were 'wheat of God' that became 'pure bread of Christ'.

Ignatius was bishop of a community that went back to the apostolic times: that of Antioch, one of the great cities of the Roman Empire. He was arrested in the reign of the emperor Trajan. On his way to Rome, where he was martyred around AD 110, he wrote pastoral letters to various Christian communities. They reveal a Christ-centred faith and theology deeply influenced by the Gospel of John and the Epistles of Paul.

Christ is truly God and truly one of us. He is truly in the Eucharist and is the bond of unity among Christians. The bishop is his special representative in the local church. Christians are called to 'newness of eternal life in Christ'. Christian death is a consummating point of that life. Ignatius asks Christians in Rome not to use influence to prevent his martyrdom because he regards himself as 'the wheat of God … to become the pure bread of Christ.'

Polycarp

One of those visited by Ignatius on his way to Rome was Polycarp, bishop of the Church in Smyrna (now Izmir in Turkey). The detailed account of Polycarp's last days, about fifty years after Ignatius, is one of the most remarkable documents of the early Church: his betrayal, his famous and moving reply when told to renounce Christ ('I have served Christ for eighty-six years and he has done me no wrong. How can I blaspheme my king who saved me?') and his death by burning in the crowded stadium.

Irenaeus, a native of what is now Turkey, Bishop of Lyons and perhaps a martyr, said of Polycarp: 'I saw him in my early years ... [he knew] many who had seen the Lord ... converted many ... declaring he had received this one and only truth from the apostles.' As someone only two generations from the Lord and probably a disciple of the apostle John, Polycarp must have been a 'cult figure' in the early Church – at least in the Asia Minor region – and seen as a living link with a very historical Christ.

Justin

From bishop in Smyrna to layman in Rome, Justin came from Nablus in Palestine, an earnest seeker of religious truth. He studied Greek philosophy at Ephesus and thought he found the answers in Plato, but one day he had a seashore conversation with an old man who introduced him to the Old Testament prophets and converted him to Christianity. He taught Christian philosophy at Ephesus, then moved to Rome and opened a school there. He devoted himself to promoting the faith by explaining it to pagans of intellectual bent; one of his explanations is addressed to the stoic emperor Antoninus Pius.

According to Justin, following the prologue of the Gospel of John, Christ is the divine and eternal Word (Logos), enlightening everyone. He sees the best of Greek philosophy ('the seeds of the Word') uniting with the Old Testament to issue into the full truth, the full revelation of the Word in Christianity. And so, Justin claims, 'Whatever has been said aright by anyone anywhere belongs to us Christians'. He insists that the Incarnation and the redemptive work of Christ, the Word made one of us, are historical facts. The 'good dreams' of the pagans really did come true.

He describes the Mass as celebrated in the Rome of his time. He teaches that the Eucharist is 'the flesh and blood of Jesus who was made man for us,' and he quotes the Last Supper words of institution. It is a joy to notice that his Mass liturgy has virtually the same shape as ours: scripture reading, homily, prayers, sign of peace, presenting of bread and wine and water, eucharistic prayer, the people's Amen, communion – and the collection! It is a lesson in Christian continuity.

About AD 165 he, along with others, was delated and arrested as a Christian. The martyrial Acts show him, supported by his companions, making a profession of faith similar to the one we use, with an emphasis on eternal life and on Christ as the fulfilment of prophecy. He is a suitable heavenly patron for Christian lay people engaged in the intellectual apostolate.

Callistus

Few popes have had as chequered a life and career as Callistus. He was born in Rome, almost certainly in the less than fashionable Trastevere ('across the Tiber'), and became a slave in the imperial household. He was convicted of embezzlement and sentenced to the mines in Sardinia. The remarkable Marcia, who combined being a Christian with being the mistress of the emperor Commodus, and who influenced her imperial partner to 'go easy' on her co-religionists, got him released. Two popes later, and by then a deacon, Callistus was elected pope himself.

He was opposed by a priest named Hippolytus, who accused him of heresy and denounced him for readmitting repentant apostates into the Church. Hippolytus was elected bishop by his supporters, thus becoming the first antipope in the history of the papacy. Callistus died a martyr's death in 222/223; murdered, it seems, by a Trastevere mob. (A reconciled Hippolytus died a martyr in 235, having been sentenced, like Callistus, to the mines in Sardinia. He composed a Eucharistic prayer which is now frequently used almost verbatim: the prayer that invokes God as 'the fountain of all holiness'.)

Cyprian

In 249 the Christians of Carthage were given a new bishop: Caecilius Thascius Cyprianus. On his conversion from paganism only three years previously he had given his wealth to the poor and vowed a life of celibacy.

Early on in his episcopate he had to cope with the short but very systematic and damaging persecution launched by the emperor Decius. His writings include an exhortation to those expecting martyrdom, a commentary on the Lord's Prayer and, most famously, a treatise on the unity of the Catholic Church. He had a spirited controversy with Pope Stephen on baptism administered outside the Church.

The emperor Valerian moved against the Church in 257. Cyprian was arrested, banished from the city and a year later brought back for trial. The Acts regarding his martyrdom depict him as a figure of aristocratic assurance and dignity: saying little, blindfolding himself, arranging a gift of gold pieces for the headsman, dying (as he wished and ensured) surrounded by his clergy and people. They end triumphantly: 'So suffered the most blessed martyr Cyprian on the eighteenth day of October *kalends* under the emperors Valerian and Gallienus in the reign of our Lord Jesus Christ to whom be honour and glory forever. Amen'. Next to Augustine, he is the most famous Latin-using North African bishop of the early Church.

> *Let's play a sort of heavenly numbers game:*
> *martyrs: philosopher one and bishops four*
> *Irenaeus, Hippolytus – two more*
> *seven passing on the flame.*

> *Seven in heaven: so the number grows*
> *but surely there's a seashore man with them*
> *to make it eight. Can we make it ten?*
> *Marcia? Commodus? Who knows?*

WITNESSES IN WORD

ATHANASIUS, JEROME, AUGUSTINE, LEO, PATRICK, BOETHIUS, BENEDICT AND GREGORY

In the fourth century the Church in the Roman Empire emerged from the catacombs. The emperor Constantine gave it civil freedom and the emperor Theodosius made Catholicism the official religion of the empire. Church authority wrestled with the strongly supported Arian doctrine that Christ was not truly God and solemnly defined his full divinity in the councils of Nicaea (325) and the first council of Constantinople (381). Roman forces wrestled with frontier-threatening tribes. For some time one of these, the Visigoths, occupied territory in the empire south of the Danube.

In the fifth century tribal peoples poured into the western half of the empire, establishing new jurisdictions and bringing about its formal collapse in 476. The eastern half was more stable, maintaining the imperial title and in the sixth century regaining some territory in the west. In these two centuries Roman and non-Roman elements fused to begin the creation of a new political and social scene in western Europe. The Church had a new mission field in Arian and pagan arrivals, and continued its conciliar teaching on Christ at Ephesus (431), Chalcedon (451) and Constantinople (553), at Ephesus also honouring Mary as 'Theotokos/God-Bearer'.

The above-mentioned 'witnesses' are of that eventful and important three-century period (c. 300–600). Here is an account of them with a focus on the remarkable word-legacy they left to Christian posterity.

Athanasius

Athanasius (c. 295–373), Bishop of Alexandria, was a central figure in the Arian crisis that convulsed the Church in the fourth century. He was with his bishop at the Council of Nicaea in 325 and succeeded him shortly afterwards. His long episcopate was punctuated by periods of being 'on the run' from his Arian enemies, including emperors and bishops. In his theology he emphasised the divinity of Christ and the reality and redemptive value of his becoming one of us. His most famous work is a biography of Saint Anthony of Egypt, the founder of Christian monasticism and an ally of his in the fight against Arianism. *Life of Anthony* by Athanasius created a new category of Christian writing. It was widely read in various languages and did much to promote the monastic ideal.

Jerome

Jerome (c. 345–420), born of Christian parents, was baptised at the age of nineteen. After scholarly travels (more or less in the footsteps of Saint Paul), in the course of which he was ordained priest, he became secretary to Pope Damasus I and spiritual director to some upper-class women in Rome. He had hopes of succeeding Damasus, but he had become unpopular in Rome and once more went east and settled in Bethlehem for the rest of his life.

He is a star of the first magnitude in the galaxy of the scriptures. His own hero was the great Origen, whose biblical commentaries he translated into Latin. His two most important achievements were the Greek-based revision of a Latin version of the four gospels (whether he revised the rest of the New Testament is disputed by scholars) and the translation of all the books of the Old Testament (a mammoth task), originally written in Hebrew, and some of the sections he came across in Aramaic and Greek. The Latin Bible, known as the Vulgate, which became the official text of the Latin-speaking part of the Church, is almost entirely the work of this one scholar, who lived up to what he had once written: 'I do what I should do in obedience to Christ who said, "search the Scriptures, seek and you shall find"'.

Augustine

Augustine (c. 354–430) is the most well-known of the Fathers of the Church and has been the most influential in the western part of the Church. After an intellectually and morally unquiet life, he was baptised in 387 and was subsequently ordained priest and bishop. His life was divided between North Africa (Tagaste, Madaura, Carthage, Hippo Regius) and Italy (Rome, Milan). His written output was immense, wide-ranging and profound. His two most famous works are *The Confessions* and *The City of God*.

In *The Confessions*, in the form of an extended prayer, he gives a history of himself: his philosophic probing, moral misdemeanours (probably exaggerated) and conversion to Christ. He gives its essential thrust in the first chapter in the well-known prayer: 'You have made us for yourself, Lord, and our heart is restless until it rests in you'. It is the most famous of all Christian autobiographies. Because of it he has been called 'the first modern man'.

He wrote *The City of God* after the sacking of Rome by the Visigoths in 410, in answer to the pagan accusation that Christianity was responsible for the collapse of Roman power and morale. He presented two separate 'loves', two value systems: the City of God (not to be identified with the Church as it historically is), whose citizens love God more than themselves, and the City of Man (not to be identified with any particular State or complex of States), whose citizens love themselves more than God. They are in conflict and competition, providing the 'horsepower' of history, the interplay of good and evil. Perhaps in this book Augustine was 'globalising' the 'two loves' he had experienced in himself and had described in *The Confessions*. This theology of history deeply influenced western thinking on the subject for centuries and still has something to say to us.

Leo

Leo I ('the Great' c. 400–461), a man of Tuscany, as he probably was, became pope in 440, at a time when the western part of the Roman empire was near extinction. He personally experienced the winds of political change in 452 when he led a delegation to Mantua in northern Italy that persuaded the fearsome Attila, king of the Huns, to withdraw beyond the Alps; as again in 455 when, though unable to stop the vandals from looting Rome, he persuaded them not to slaughter and burn.

He was very conscious of being the successor of Peter ('in his place we act') and of the status of the people he pastured:

'Christian, realise your dignity: sharer in the divine nature ... snatched from the power of darkness, brought into the light and kingdom of God, through baptism made the temple of the Holy Spirit. Do not let depravity expel so great a Dweller ... your price is the blood of Christ.'

This passage comes from a superb series of doctrine-rich sermons on the life of Christ from Christmas to Ascension: 'The Word made flesh was already dwelling among us and Christ had devoted himself totally to restoring the human race'. His most famous piece is the *Tome of Leo*, a letter to the patriarch of Constantinople. With authoritative assurance he announced it as 'the teaching of the Catholic Church on the Incarnation of Our Lord Jesus Christ':

> Christ is one Person, the eternal Word/Son, truly God, in nature truly divine. Through the Holy Spirit and Mary this Person is also truly human. Each nature is distinct from the other, remaining complete and intact but both natures are harmoniously united in the one Person. 'This same eternal Only-Begotten of the Father was born of the Holy Spirit and the Virgin Mary. This birth in time neither contributed to nor diminished the eternal divine birth but attended totally to the restoring of humankind ... The Holy Spirit gave fecundity to the Virgin, a real body was taken from a body and ... the Word was made flesh and dwelt amongst us, that is, in that flesh which the Word took from a human being and made alive with a spirit of rational life.'

The Council of Chalcedon acclaimed the Tome ('Peter has spoken through Leo') and issued a doctrine-defining statement in keeping with it. Leo is very much the Pope of the Incarnation.

Patrick

Patrick (fifth century), apostle of Ireland. Many things about this towering figure in Irish tradition are historically uncertain. The essential Patrick and the shape of his life and apostolate are found in his *Confession*, a very personalised defence of his mission, which he wrote before he died.

It gives details of his Romano-British background, capture, enslavement, escape, spiritual experiences, missionary return, apostolic successes and personal dangers.The portrait is of a humble, fearless and practical man, wonderingly thankful for God's choice of him, delighted and astonished at the response of so many to his message. He was especially concerned for convert enslaved women, tenaciously devoted to the 'people whom the Lord has gained at the uttermost parts of the earth,' deciding, as by Christ's command, to 'be with them till the end of my life'. And so it is in Ireland, after fifteen centuries, that his remains still rest.

Boethius

Boethius (c. 480–524) was in the service of the Ostrogothic king Theodoric, who controlled much of Italy. He was accused of treason and was executed after a long imprisonment.

Through his writings, this bridge-figure between Greco-Roman and medieval cultures was a major influence on the European mind. His most famous work was the *De Consolatione Philophiae/Concerning the Consolation of Philosophy*, in which, among other things, he examined the human psyche and its search for and fulfilment in God. Written in prison in the shadow of death and echoing Plato and Augustine, it was staple reading of educated Europeans for centuries. Its translators included Alfred the Great, Geoffrey Chaucer and Elizabeth Tudor.

Benedict

Benedict (c. 480–546) was born in Norcia in central Italy and educated in Rome. He became a hermit in a mountainous area near Rome and was joined by other solitaries. He brought his companions to Monte Cassino between Rome and Naples and there founded what was to become the most famous monastery in Europe.

The most historically significant thing he did at Monte Cassino was to write a rule. He based it to some extent on an older rule or rules, but in its essential thrust, its moderation and humaneness, its concept of an abbot who himself is subject to the rule and its distinctive treatment of various elements of monastic life, it can be taken as the work of Benedict. Its first word is 'Listen'. One of its key statements is: 'Let absolutely nothing be preferred to Christ'. It can be seen, or listened to, as the spelling out of the Benedictine motto 'Peace'.

Variously nuanced, in time it became the basic text of monastic life in Europe, earning for Benedict the title of patriarch of monasticism in the west, and indirectly helping the cultural and material development of the continent. It has been called Europe's first written constitution.

Gregory

Gregory I ('the Great' c. 540–604), a Roman aristocrat, was prefect of the city of Rome for a few years, superintending its maintenance and safety. He turned his elegant home into a monastery dedicated to Saint Andrew and became a monk himself. Ordained deacon, he served as papal representative at the imperial court in Constantinople and as papal counsellor. In 590 he was chosen pope by acclamation.

With the Lombards in north Italy threatening what was officially imperial territory (including Rome) and the Constantinople government powerless and incompetent, Gregory kept them at bay by buying them off. He thus became a (reluctant) political ruler: a development that helped to lead a century and a half later to the creation of the Papal States.

The money for the Lombards came from the revenues of the papally owned estates in Italy and elsewhere. Gregory was concerned that the poor and needy should benefit from them too. He saw himself as their steward rather than as their landlord; this was one way to be 'servant of the servants of God', as he liked to call himself.

While asserting his own primacy, he respected the rights of the bishops, practising what would be called today 'the principle of subsidiarity'. One famous direct intervention of his was the sending of monks of Saint Andrew's monastery, led by their prior Augustine, to England to evangelise the Anglo-Saxons who had invaded Britain after the withdrawal of the Romans.

Our Mass liturgy still bears his stamp: the prayer for peace and salvation in the first Eucharistic Prayer just before the words of institution, the present position of the Our Father, a handful of prefaces and many prayer texts are of his doing.

He was a prolific writer: homilies based on Scripture; the Book of Morals, a commentary on the Book of Job and also an encyclopaedia of Christian doctrine; the Pastoral Care for bishops and priests; the Dialogues, a miscellany for popular consumption of saints' lives; and the letters, a mine of information on his times and his own personality. Few popes, if any, have left as impressive a legacy of personally written works.

Scholar, bishops, missioner
a monk, two popes, a prisoner
new peoples, half an empire gone
God's City stays, the Lord lives on.
These eight believe the future's his
they know he'll keep his promises
and so they write their legacy
pass on the truth that makes us free.

WHITE MARTYRS

COLMCILLE, COLUMBANUS, GALL AND KILIAN

'Red martyrdom' – the sacrificing of oneself in death in utter witness and loving loyalty to Christ – was a very evident reality in the early Church. The related concept of 'white martyrdom' began to develop. Irish monks described it as 'giving up what you love for the love of Christ'. It found a remarkable expression from the sixth to the ninth century in the Irish penitential and apostolic outreach to Britain, Iceland and mainland Europe. To relinquish the security of kin, native culture and environment to brave, apostolically, the unknown and dangerous was surely a special witness to Christ that could be called martyrdom. Perhaps it can be seen as an imitation of the great Patrick himself; or as an engracement of the wanderlust deep in the Irish psyche (Strabo of Reichenau, the biographer of Gall, noted that 'wandering' was a 'second nature of the Irish race'). Here is an account of four 'white martyrs'.

Colmcille
Colmcille ('Dove of the Church') was of the royal Uí Néill dynasty, born at Gartan in Donegal. He studied at Glasnevin near the Ford of the Hurdles (the well in the Dublin hills dedicated to him may be related to his time in Liffeyland) and at Clonard under the great Finnian and, it seems, did something of a monastic tour of Ireland. He founded monasteries at Derry and Durrow (the place names seem to indicate a fondness for oak trees) and at Kells (where he is named with Patrick on the great cross).

In 563 he departed for Scotland and established a monastery on the island of Iona, which became a missionary and cultural centre for Scotland and northern England. Whether his going was a pure act of white martyrdom or an act of penance for his part in bringing about a battle in which many died is not clear; it was probably a blend of the two. He died in 597, the very year in which Augustine of Rome landed at the other end of Britain to evangelise the Anglo-Saxons – an example of Christian linkage and continuity.

Like Patrick, Colmcille became an iconic figure in Irish tradition: the 'white martyr' par excellence; priest, prince, peacemaker, poet; and linked to Patrick and Brigid at the head of the Irish sanctoral. Not all of the Colmcille lore is historical, but behind it is indubitably a great personality. A work of his hand, in a very literal sense, may still be with us: the handwriting in the ancient psalter, called the '*Cathach*' because the Uí Néill carried it into battle as a morale-booster and for protection. This national treasure is in Dublin, only a street away from where an even greater treasure, the most beautiful gospel book in the world, the Book of Kells, probably written mostly at Iona, is enshrined and contemplated.

'Dove': surely not the name
for all that style, that royalty
that swept through Ireland like a flame
and braved the northern sea.

'Eagle', perhaps: soaring high
symbol of power, of master-will
lord of mountain, wind and sky
bird imperial.

Back to tradition: keep the dove
(a sign of the Spirit, don't forget)
but add a word denoting love
why not 'passionate'?

Columbanus

Columbanus was the doyen of the Irish missionary movement in early medieval Europe. This Leinsterman was a monk of the great monastery of Bangor on the shore of Belfast Lough. In 590/591 he left Bangor for the European mainland with twelve companions. In Burgundy he founded monasteries at Luxeuil, Annagray and Fontaines, which in turn produced 'daughter' houses. He attacked immorality among clergy and laity; by censuring the king he predictably got himself expelled. After some time on monastic mission in the Zurich-Lake Constance area, he crossed the Alps to northern Italy where he founded his most famous monastery at Bobbio, north-east of Genoa. He lived there until his death in 615. His remains rest in the church named after him.

His writings, some of them verse, are an important part of medieval Latin literature of Irish provenance. They include lyrical passages rather reminiscent of John of the Cross. His biographer, Jonas of Bobbio, says that many of his pieces were suitable for song. One wonders if they were sung to Irish melodies.

He wrote: 'My desire was to visit the pagans and that the gospel be preached to them by us'. In a letter to Pope Gregory the Great regarding the dating of Easter, he uses the phrase '*totius Europae*' (of all Europe). These two quotes together indicate that he had a sense of Europe as a 'unity' that was largely in urgent need of the gospel and grace of Christ. We can reasonably claim Columbanus as the most European of Irish saints.

Leinster man who travelled north
Bangor, then adventured forth
Luxeuil, Fontaines and Bobbio
the Rhine, the Trebbia, the Po
Lake Constance, Alps and Appennines
Roman roads, fields full of vines
names that map the way you went
pilgrim to a continent
man of Spartan holiness
admonishing the pope, no less
and in your heart God's fountain flows
the fire of giving ever glows
keep Europe in your blessed ken
lest pagan darkness come again
Amen, amen.

Gall

Gall left Bangor with Columbanus in 590/591 and accompanied him as far as the Lake Constance area. There he stayed for the rest of his life as the 'holy man' and apostle of the region. The great abbey of Sankt Gallen was built on the site of his hermitage. He and Columbanus never met after the latter's departure for Italy, but he was acquainted with the Bobbio monk Jonas and no doubt contributed to his biography of the great man.

Columbanus has a continent to pray for
I know him quite a bit
so I'm sure he's up to it.

It's the canton of Saint Gallen that I pray for
it's wonderful to feel
that my prayer is en famille.

Kilian

Kilian (c. 640–689) is proudly claimed by the people of Mullagh in County Cavan as one of their own; their parish church is dedicated to him. He led a missionary contingent to Würzburg in south-west Germany. Among his converts was the duke of the region, who he persuaded to separate from his mistress, who was also his brother's widow. The scorned sister-in-law, playing Herodias to Kilian's John the Baptist, had him and two fellow missionaries murdered. The Neumünster in Würzburg houses the enshrined remains of the Irish trio, whose white martyrdom turned to red.

Würzburg: far from a Cavan sky
far from a drumlin scene
far from the western sea
stretching endlessly.

Würzburg: here is my place to die
thanks, Lord, for all that's been
God's ocean: Trinity
loving endlessly.

THE MAN OF ONE PLACE

BEDE

Next time you are on Tyneside, visit the town of Jarrow, find the church of Saint Paul and look at the memorial stone of the monastery church that once stood there. Its Latin inscription, translated into the language derived at least partly from the language of those who made the stone and saw it set in place, runs as follows:

> Dedication of the Basilica of Saint Paul on the ninth of the Kalends of May in the fifteenth year of King Egfrid, the fourth year of Abbot Ceolfrid, builder under God of the same church.

Among those present on that Sunday, 23 April 685, was almost certainly a boy of about thirteen who was to be the intellectual 'star' of the early English Church and one of the greatest of Church historians: Bede of Jarrow (c. 672/673–735).

A few years before his death, as he concluded his famous Church history, he wrote of himself: his birth on the lands of the two-house monastery of Wearmouth and Jarrow; his monastic schooling and life as a monk, deacon and priest; and his delight in learning, teaching and writing. He gives a long list of his works on various subjects. Thanks to Benedict Biscop, the founder abbot of Wearmouth-Jarrow, and his successor Ceolfrid, the monastery was rich with books. These were the tools of his trade: teaching himself from 'venerable Fathers' like Augustine, Ambrose, Jerome and Gregory; teaching his brethren, local people and doubtless others in quest of enlightenment; or writing for those farther afield in place and time.

This man of one place, coming to his fiftieth year, could look back over a momentous century in the religious history of his time: the Roman mission in the south under Augustine of Canterbury and Birinus; the Celtic mission in the north under Aidan of Iona and Lindisfarne; the refusal of the Welsh bishops to assist in the conversion of the Angles and Saxons from across the sea who had dispossessed their people; and the controversy over the dating of Easter with the Roman system prevailing at the convention of Whitby.

It was the time of personalities like the royal church-women Etheldreda and Hilda, the church-men Colman, Wilfrid and Cuthbert of Lindisfarne (perhaps also of Mulhuddart, in the present Co. Dublin), and the kings Edwin, Oswald and Egfried (donor of the lands of Wearmouth-Jarrow). It was the era in which the faith was established and the Church was organised in England.

Albinus, Abbot of Canterbury, urged Bede to record this important period and he obliged by writing the work on which his fame predominantly rests: *The Ecclesiastical History of the English People*. He rates high as a historian. He makes the most of his impressive 'cast'. He is careful about facts and chronology and has a sense of dramatic event. He sees history as having a moral as well as an informative value.

As regards chronology, he dates events as '*anno Domini*' (in the year of the Lord). He takes as his starting point the birth year of Christ according to the (somewhat incorrect) reckoning of the fifth or sixth century Dionysius Exiguus (Dennis the Little). *The History* is the first major historical work in which this date system is consistently used. It set a headline which in time was adopted world-wide. In this respect the man of one place has travelled extensively. Think of Bede next time you date a letter or buy a calendar.

He had a high regard for Ireland. He praised the hospitality of Irish monasteries to English students, acknowledged the Irish contribution to the conversion of England (one of his heroes is Aidan of Iona and Lindisfarne, who preached the gospel in Northumbria and whose only defect was to favour the Celtic way of dating Easter!) and disapproved of King Egfrid's military exploits in Ireland: 'That nation which has always been friendly to the English'. Bede might well serve as a patron saint of Anglo-Irish relations.

The generally accepted year of his death is 735. A pupil of his, Cuthbert (afterwards an abbot), gives a graphic eye-witness account of his last days, describing how he felt death approaching and cheerfully (*hilariter*) continued to teach and dictate, distributed small gifts to the brethren, asked for Masses and prayers, ensured that the last chapter and sentence of the book being completed were written, thanked God for his life and looked forward to seeing 'Christ my King in his glory'.

'So lying on the floor of his cell he sang "Glory be to the Father and to the Son and to the Holy Spirit" and when he had named the Holy Spirit he breathed his last breath'.

I am a blessed man
my work is my delight
I pray, I teach, I write
beside the German sea.

I have a master plan
a book of special grace
the christening of my race
and dated all AD.

I call upon your name:
Lord, bless your Englishry
past, present, still to be
shine your face on them.

And others have a claim
they share these island lands
Lord, hold them in your hands
Amen, amen, amen.

LOVE STORY

ELIZABETH

About one hundred and sixty miles south-west of Berlin is the historic town of Eisenach. On a rocky height overlooking the town is the Wartburg, for centuries the stronghold of the ruler of this part of Germany. The best-known resident of the Wartburg in its long history is Martin Luther, who was brought there for protection when he was excommunicated by the Church and outlawed by the Holy Roman Empire of the German Nation. Visitors can still see the room where he translated part of the Bible and, it is alleged, threw an ink bottle at the devil.

Three centuries earlier the Wartburg had a resident rather different to Luther, but like him destined to be important in the religious history of Germany.

Elizabeth of Hungary (1207–1231) was the daughter of Andrew II of Hungary and Gertrude of Andechs-Meran. At the age of four she was betrothed to Ludwig, son and heir to the *Landgrave* or Count of Thuringia, and came to the Wartburg to grow up with her future husband and to be groomed as the future First Lady (*Landgravine*) of the principality. Her mother-in-law to be was a loving foster mother and Ludwig proved an ideal fiancé: lovable and loving and suitably attentive.

They were married when she was fourteen and he was twenty or twenty-one and by then *Landgrave*. Theirs was not one of those royal marriages that are politically convenient yet humanly disastrous. They were deeply in love, with most of the passion, it seems, coming from her. There is a delightful picture of Ludwig holding her hands as she began her night prayers with him falling asleep, as she prayed on with his hands still joined to hers. They had three children: Hermann, Sophia and Gertrude.

She had spiritual children too: the sick and poor of the principality. In her care for them Ludwig was lovingly supportive. 'Her charities will gain us divine blessing,' he said, 'let her give to God whatever she wants to give so long as he leaves me the

Wartburg and the Neumburg.' But far more than the loss of earthly goods was soon to be asked of them.

In 1227 that most alarming and enigmatic of medieval monarchs, the emperor Frederick II, proceeded to launch his long-awaited crusade against the Turks in the Holy Land. In feudal duty to his emperor, Ludwig set off with his contingent of crusaders and met 'Stupor Mundi' (the Wonder of the World), as Frederick was sometimes known, in southern Italy. The crusading forces embarked but fever broke out on board the ships and they returned to port. Ludwig was one of the fever victims who died in Brindisi.

When Elizabeth realised that he was dead her grief was uncontrollable. The years of paradise she had with him had come to an end. The light had gone out. Not long afterwards she and her children left the Wartburg. Why she left is not entirely clear; the traditional account puts it down to in-law hostility. The local people (though surely not the sick and poor) rejected her. An aunt who was an abbess and an uncle who was a bishop relieved her need and she moved to Marburg in the principality of Hesse, which bordered on Thuringia.

She was drawn to a life of poverty and dedication to the sick and poor. Having provided for her children, she became a member of the Third Order of Saint Francis, with an emphasis on penance. As she had done near the Wartburg, she established a hospice or hospital in Marburg where the residents became her new family.

Conrad of Marburg had succeeded a Franciscan as her spiritual guide. One suspects that her deep desires and his direction did not always entirely coincide – Hungarian passion for freedom versus German passion for law perhaps? He knew that he had a saint on his hands. After her death he called her 'consoler of the poor' and 'restorer of the famine stricken', and said 'before God' that he had rarely seen 'a more contemplative woman'.

On her deathbed she told him that everything she owned was to be given to the poor, except the plain dress she was wearing, in which she wished to be buried: 'She received the body of the Lord and then until evening frequently spoke of the good things she had heard in sermons. Finally, commending herself and all around her to God with great devotion, she died as if gently falling asleep'.

She died on 16/17 November 1231, aged twenty-four. She was canonised only four years later. Her tomb became a place of pilgrimage. In the religious divisions of the sixteenth century Hesse officially converted to Protestantism and its Count Philip (a strong adherent of Martin Luther), who disapproved of pilgrimages and the invocation of saints, had the remains removed to a secret place, which has never been discovered. In so doing he unwittingly gave her a new and posthumous identification with the poor, whose graves are so often unmarked and ignored.

> *A love not just for two but for three and four*
> *and five and six and seven and many more*
> *all caught into a Love with a capital 'L'*
> *from whom all gifts and graces shine and spring*
> *of whom all things of power and beauty sing*
> *in whom eternally all shall be well.*

THE DYER'S DAUGHTER

CATHERINE

Siena on its three hills between Florence and Rome is one of the most beautiful cities in Italy. It is mainly famous for two things: a school of painting and a woman – the elegant pre-Renaissance art of men like Ducci and Martini and a dyer's daughter named Catherine Benincasa.

Catherine was born in 1347 (the date generally accepted) into the very large family of Giacomo Benincasa and Monna Lapa Piagenti. There are stories of childhood prayers and penances and she is said to have had a vision of Christ in glory at the age of five or six. As she approached the age of marriage (in that society it was taken for granted that a young woman either married or became a nun) she took part in the social life expected of her, but only for a while – she made it clear that she did not intend to marry. There was family uproar and even persecution, but her father had second thoughts about his unusual daughter. He gave orders that she was to be allowed to live her own life.

That extraordinary life turned out to be a blend of prayer, mystical experience, penance and pain; lived almost entirely in a room at the top of the house. She attended the nearby Dominican church and became a member of the Dominican Third Order. She learned to read, discovered the Bible and steeped herself in the psalms and the epistles of Saint Paul. Then, mystically directed, she began to interact again with her family and the outside world. She became a familiar figure in the Santa Della Scala, the great charity complex of Siena (hospital-cum-hospice-cum-foundling home) and a social centre too; a great place for meeting people and swapping news. Perhaps La Scala was Catherine's ladder to Avignon and Rome.

In a development which became a conversation point in Siena salons, this young woman, neither wife nor nun, unschooled in the conventional sense, became the centre of a circle of devotees, learners and disciples in the Christian life: men and women, priests, religious, layfolk, young and old. They were fascinated by her insight and intuition in spiritual matters. She became an icon to them. The mockers and critics called them '*Caterinati*'.

Criticism then turned to accusation to such an extent that the Dominicans put her on the agenda of their general chapter in 1374. She was given a favourable verdict and an officially appointed spiritual director: Raimondo Della Vigne, who afterwards became Dominican Master General. Thus affirmed and supported, she focused on matters papal, both political and spiritual.

She launched what might be called a crusade by correspondence in support of the crusade favoured by Pope Gregory XI against the Turks, who were pushing through south-east Europe. She took part in the negotiations to end a war between certain Italian city-states and the Papal States; her effort involved a visit to Avignon, a papal enclave on the edge of what was then France, where the Popes had been living since 1309. Like many others, Catherine thought that it was high time for Roman papal presence to be restored.

Pope Gregory XI probably thought so too but he procrastinated. He certainly paid attention to (and was probably rather intimidated by) this young woman, who bombarded him with letters to which he replied by notes and verbal messages (the Gregory-Catherine dialogue must be unique in papal history). He left Avignon in September 1377 and arrived in Rome in January 1378. Catherine and her followers rejoiced – but not for long.

Gregory died on 27 March 1378. On 8 April, with the Roman crowd demanding a Roman Pope, a conclave of sixteen cardinals (ten of them French) elected the southern Italian Archbishop of Bari (not a cardinal) as Urban VI. An austere man himself, he made it clear to the cardinals that high thinking and plain living would be enforced, and that their wings of power which had been spread at Avignon would be clipped. His bad manners made the message even more unpalatable.

The French cardinals withdrew from Rome and were joined by others. The dissident cardinals declared that the election of Urban had not been free and was therefore invalid. Most of them elected Robert of Geneva as Clement VII, who took up residence at Avignon. The Great Western Schism, which was to last until 1417, had begun.

Even before the final break Catherine was counselling Urban to promote Church reform and control his temper. After the break he summoned her to Rome and there she spent the last year and a half of her life, advising the difficult pontiff, pouring out letter after letter on his behalf, praying and agonising for her wounded and beloved Church.

Shortly before she died she dictated the spiritual testament of her life, the famous *Dialogue*. God is the One who is. God's love is creative and re-creative. Christ is the bridge by which we cross to life. His blood is the expression of the divine love: 'Eternal Trinity, you are the Maker. I am the made. And you have enlightened me to realise that in your re-making of me through the blood of your only-begotten Son you fell in love with the beauty of what you made'.

She died on 29 April 1380. Not long before, in the nightmare of the schism, she had renewed her faith in and love of the Church, 'that sweet Bride' giving 'strength and light', in whom is 'the gate of the crucified Christ', our essential escort into 'the joy in the beauty of God in the depths of the Trinity.' 'Eternal God, accept my life as a sacrifice for the mystical body of Holy Church'.

> *Church: Christ's deed*
> *but wounded, in need*
> *Bride of his Heart*
> *now let me start*
> *to bring her to bliss*
> *because she is his.*

MEDIEVAL MOSAIC

FROM EDWIN TO JOAN

First, a roll call of royalty: rulers who brought their personal faith to bear on their political life. The Anglo-Saxons are foremost in this. Edwin of Northumbria opened his kingdom to the faith. However, the Christian mission collapsed when he was killed in 633 in battle against the pagan Penda of Mercia and his ally Cadwallon. His cousin Oswald claimed the crown, defeated Cadwallon and became the partner of Aidan of Iona and Lindisfarne in the re-conversion of his kingdom. He died in battle against Penda, his last words a prayer for his fallen soldiers. The cousins were honoured as martyrs and are heroes of Bede in his *Ecclesiastical History of the English People*.

Edmund of East Anglia died for his faith and his people at the hands of the Danes, who were harassing his kingdom. His cult was widespread and his tomb at Bury-Saint Edmunds remained a place of pilgrimage for centuries.

A contemporary of Edmund was Alfred of Wessex, known as Alfred the Great. His defeat and containment of the Danes and the widespread acceptance of his rule beyond Wessex were an important part of the process towards a unitary English monarchy. He developed the religious and cultural life of his people, maintaining contact with Rome, promoting education and providing English translations of Latin texts, thus beginning English prose literature; he was quite a writer himself. He led a thoughtful, prayerful and austere life in which daily Mass was the norm.

Edgar the Peaceful was of the Alfred mould. His coronation set a precedent in that it was a definite liturgy, a consecration of the sovereign. He was remembered as a 'holy king'. His son and successor Edward achieved official sainthood: his death by murder, while he was still in his teens, was considered martyrdom.

From England we move on to mainland Europe. 'Good king Wenceslaus' (c. 907–935) of the Christmas carol, Duke of Bohemia, had a practically pagan mother (a Lady Macbeth figure who instigated the murder of his grandmother), a brother with his eye on the ducal succession and a society in tension between Christians and pagans. Against this difficult background the young duke worked hard for peace and the Church. Tradition presents him as devoted to the Blessed Sacrament and to the poor. After the birth of his son he was murdered by his brother and his accomplices (the brother afterwards repented and retired into a monastery). At once regarded as a martyr, Wenceslaus/Vaclav is the chief patron saint of Bohemia, and his tomb in Prague is still a place of pilgrimage.

On Christmas day 1000, Stephen/Istvan, ruler of Hungary, convert from paganism, was crowned with a crown donated, at his request, by the Pope; a dramatic signal of his resolve to make his country a Christian kingdom in the heart of Europe. He enlisted Benedictines to make his dream a reality. He is said to have dedicated Hungary to Our Lady: it came to be called the Kingdom of Mary. He is its patron saint. He told his son: 'In the royal palace at the Church, first planted by Christ our Head, holds second place after the faith'. He exhorted him to various virtues: 'These endow the royal crown: without them no one can reign here or reach the eternal kingdom'. The crown of Stephen, worn by his successors over the centuries, is still a national and deeply symbolic treasure.

Stephen's brother-in-law, Henry of Bavaria, Emperor of the Germanies and King of Italy, exercised considerable control over the Church in his realm and was intent on its reform. Olaf of Norway, a convert from paganism, zealous for the faith and killed in battle fighting for his crown, achieved instant canonisation in the Scandinavian world.

Louis IX of France (1226–1270) really described his own style of kingship in his instruction to his son and heir: 'Take part in the worship of the Church … pray to the Lord in speech or in meditation of heart … be just towards your subjects … more towards the poor than towards the rich until you are certain of the truth … take care that all your subjects have justice and peace.'

Next, a montage of monks, friars and bishops. Martin I (649–655) is unique in papal history as the only pope martyred, not by a pagan, but by a Christian emperor. He convoked a council that condemned the monothelitism (the doctrine that Christ Incarnate had only one will) favoured by the Byzantine Emperor Constans II. Already ill, he was arrested at the altar of his cathedral, brought to Constantinople, convicted of treason and exiled to the Crimea, where he died of the appalling maltreatment endured after arrest and trial.

Bede of Jarrow wrote the famous *Ecclesiastical History of the English People*. His contemporary fellow Englishman Winfrid-Boniface organised the Church in Germany, stressing union with the papacy and promoting the monastic life, and helped in Church reform in Frankland. The German bishops still confer annually at Fulda, where his remains rest and where the slashed gospel-book is kept, which tradition says he held while being stabbed to death with his companions in Frisia in 754 (the scene of his first mission many years before).

In the following century, the brothers Cyril and Methodius from Greece (then part of the Byzantine empire) came as missionaries to 'greater Moravia' in central Europe at its ruler's request. With papal approval they introduced vernacular liturgy in Slavonic. After Cyril's death, Methodius continued his mission, despite opposition from those who favoured a Latin-using Church. The brothers are patrons of Christian unity and are important in the history of Slavic literature.

The Church of the later eleventh century had a papal giant in Gregory VII (Hildebrand). With a vision of the Church as 'free, chaste and Catholic' and of the papacy as representing the lordship of Christ, he waged war on simony, clerical marriage and immorality and royal appointments of unsuitable personnel to prelacies. His chief antagonist was Henry IV of Germany, who was hardly the 'lover of justice' that Gregory said every Catholic king should be. This excommunicated monarch asking Gregory for absolution at Canossa is one of the great dramatic moments of the medieval Church.

Bernard of Clairvaulx was a dominant figure in the twelfth-century Church: populariser of the Cistercians, theologian and mystic (and suspicious of the new scholasticism), crusade preacher and (sometimes overly severe) defender of the faith. He stressed God as Love, the Lord's humanity, Our Lady's role in the Christ-event. He and Malachy of Armagh were co-founders of the first Cistercian house in Ireland in 1142: Mellifont in the present County Louth, on land donated by Donnchad Cerbaill, King of Oirgialla, associate of Malachy in his Church reform work.

The poor man of Assisi, Francis Bernardone (1182–1226), challenged Christians (especially the affluent) of his time with his radical following of the Lord in poverty, simplicity of life, joy of spirit and delight in God's creation. (He would be a splendid heavenly patron for Christians concerned about the environment: his *Canticle of the Sun*, a gem of Italian literature, set to music, would be an inspiring anthem for them.) He still challenges and attracts. One of his followers was Anthony of Lisbon, who was to become Anthony of Padua and one of the most popular of saints, patron of many causes and honorary admiral of the Portuguese navy.

Dominic de Guzman (1170–1221), a canon of the Spanish dioceses of Osma and a man with a great capacity for friendship and a passion for truth, was alarmed by the inroads of the Albigensian movement with its denial of the goodness of material creation and its consequent rejection of the Incarnation and sacramental system. He founded the Order of Preachers to defend and pass on the faith they had contemplated: *contemplata tradere*.

Thomas Aquinas certainly lived up to this Dominican ideal: he was an immense influence in the intellectual history of the Church with a theology that was a profound meditation on dogma and a realist philosophy that respected matter and sense as well as spirit.

Two lesser-known communicators of contemplated truth were Hermann, monk of the island abbey of Reichenau in Lake Constance, and Aelred, abbot of the Cistercian abbey of Rievaulx in north Yorkshire. Hermann, crippled in body, brilliant in mind and charming in personality, shone as a teacher in various subjects. He may have written (words and music) the exquisite *Alma*

Redemptoris Mater and *Salve Regina* ('Mother of the Redeemer' and 'Hail, Holy Queen'). Aelred wrote a very famous work called *De Amicitia Spirituali* ('Of Spiritual Friendship') with its opening statement: 'You and I, and I hope that Christ will be the third'.

A few years after Aelred's death in 1167, Archbishop Thomas Becket was murdered in his cathedral in Canterbury and Archbishop Laurence Ó Toole tried to allay the storm of Norman invasion and Irish defence, while the winds of historic change whirled around his cathedral of Christchurch in Dublin.

Finally, a resplendent regiment of witnessing women. Ludmilla was the wife of the first Christian duke of Bohemia and like him was baptised by the great Methodius. She promoted Christianity among her people and instructed her grandson Wenceslaus/Vaclav in the faith. Jealous of this, his pro-pagan mother Drahomira instigated her murder. Grandmother and grandson are patron martyr-saints of Bohemia.

Margaret, Hungarian-English princess, became the wife of Malcolm III of Scotland (the Malcolm mentioned in *Macbeth*), whom she first met after she was shipwrecked off the Scottish coast. She was a lady bountiful to the needy of her adopted country and, aided by Malcolm and Lanfranc of Canterbury, did much for its religious and cultural life.

Clare of Assisi, friend and follower of Francis and co-founder of the Second Franciscan Order, focused her life on the Blessed Sacrament and on the Church as the Body of Christ. In Germany the mystics Mechtilde and Gertrude were messengers of the Sacred Heart and have an important place in the history of the devotion. The Benedictine abbess Hildegarde of Bingen was a phenomenal polymath: mystic, counsellor, writer with a vast output of letters and pieces on various subjects, religious and secular. Zita of Lucca spent nearly all her life as a servant in the one house, finding God in Mass, prayer, penance, chores and those she met. Like Hildegarde, she had the gift of counselling. She is the patron saint of domestic workers.

The married life of Elizabeth of Hungary was a fairy-tale idyll. Not so the married life of her name-sake and grand-niece Elizabeth of Portugal: enduring the errancy of her husband the king, caring for his extra-marital children as for her own, keeping the peace between him and their difficult son. Her peace-making extended into Iberian politics. Like her grand-aunt Elizabeth, she was good to the poor and became a Franciscan tertiary. In her apostolate of peace she was certainly a true Franciscan.

Bridget of Sweden, mother and mystic, founder of the Bridgettines, combined her prayer and penance and care for the poor with a concern for a wounded Church; in this active concern she was a counterpart of her contemporary Catherine of Siena. She is the patron saint of Sweden. Another contemporary was Julian of Norwich of *Revelations of Divine Love*. In her account of the experience she compares God's love to a mother's love and pays tribute to the 'little and the simple', who in innocence respond to that love. Was she thinking here of Jesus and the children? Her message is still powerful.

In the fifteenth century an illiterate teenage girl saved the French monarchy and state. Joan of Arc is a patron saint of France and the most famous woman in its history – indeed one of the most famous women in the history of Europe. She died a most dreadful death as the victim of an unholy alliance between local Church authority and power politics. Out of the flames and smoke in the marketplace in Rouen on 30 May 1431, her last prayer could be heard: 'Jesu!' repeated again and again.

A great procession honouring the Lord
from eastern borderlands to western seas
shaping a continent through centuries
people of the Word.

At work, at play, at prayer, in town and field
clergy in choir and kings in battle-din
seekers and finders of God without, within
people Spirit-sealed.

Francis, Dominic, Bernard, Bridget, Clare
Hermann, Laurence, Julian, many more
come to know the Lord, to thank, adore
come to give, to dare.

Women called to royal court and throne
Zita: keeping house from day to day
Joan: Rouen, the thirtieth of May
meets her king, goes home.

LONDONER

THOMAS

In Chelsea there is a mulberry tree that has for many people a special significance. The tradition is that it was there in the sixteenth century on the estate of a distinguished Londoner who was a hero of the Catholic faith and that it was a venue for him and his family and friends to meet. Nearby a statue of him overlooks the Thames with the iscription: 'Thomas More, Scholar, Statesman, Saint'.

He was born in London in 1477/1478 of, as he wrote himself, a family 'not illustrious but of honourable standing'. His father, a lawyer, secured him, after some local schooling, a place as a servant-pupil in the Lambeth household of John Morton, Archbishop of Canterbury and Lord Chancellor of England. Morton's successor as chancellor had his first contact with high society in Church and State in the place where he was to make his stand for Church against State.

After Lambeth and a sequence of Oxford legal training and public life, he entered the royal service. The king welcomed him to court, giving him the motto, 'Look first to God and then to me', and honoured him with a knighthood.

His scholarly interests and contacts made him something of an international figure. He published quite a few books, including the famous *Utopia*, which is mainly a satire on contemporary society, in ways prophetic. He considered the religious and priestly life but finally opted for marriage. He married twice and had four children by his first marriage. He lived first in Bucklesbury and then moved to Chelsea. He presided punctiliously over his household, emphasising education and prayer. Daily Mass and much prayer was his own personal regime. He was especially close to his daughter Margaret; to her he entrusted the washing of his hair shirt.

An author of the time described him as: 'A man of angel's wit and singular learning ... of marvellous mirth and pastimes and sometimes of a sad gravity ... A man for all seasons.' Gravity rather than mirth marks the portrait by Hans Holbein, painted around 1527. Perhaps the gravity is connected with the great question beginning to demand attention at that time: was the king married or was he not?

Henry, Duke of York, had become heir to the throne at the death of his brother Arthur. Shortly after his accession as Henry VIII, he married Arthur's widow Catherine of Aragon by papal dispensation from the impediment of affinity. (In the canon law of that time this impediment derived from sexual intercourse, not from the marriage itself.) The dispensation was given on the supposition or at least the possibility that the Arthur-Catherine marriage had been consummated.

The Henry-Catherine marriage was dogged by miscarriages, stillbirths and deaths in infancy. Only one child survived: Mary. Henry became desperate for a male heir to ensure, as he and many others saw it, the stability of the dynasty and the State. He professed misgivings, probably genuine, about the validity of the dispensation: was not the loss of so many children a punishment for transgressing a divine law that the Church could not dispense from? And had the reasons given to obtain the dispensation been true? Then his 'fatal attraction' had appeared: Anne Boleyn, maid of honour to Catherine, ambitious to be wife and queen.

Henry consulted More at least twice about the marriage. More felt unable in conscience to support the petition for an annulment. The king's Lord Chancellor, the flamboyant and ambitious Cardinal Wolsey, did so petition the irresolute and politically conscious Clement VII. Clement appointed him and Cardinal Campeggio, distinguished canonist and absentee Bishop of Salisbury, to try the case in London. Catherine refused to recognise the court as impartial and insisted that her marriage of six months to the fourteen- or fifteen-year-old Arthur had not been consummated. Clement revoked the case to Rome. The court adjourned without passing judgment. The furious Henry dismissed Wolsey and appointed More Lord Chancellor in October 1529.

So began the 1530s: that unique decade in the religious history of England when the nation, in obedience to its king, ceased to be part of the Catholic world. In 1531 the clergy recognised Henry as the Supreme Head of the Church in his realm 'so far as the law of Christ allows'. In 1532 they surrendered their legislative independence to the king and More resigned his chancellorship. In the following year, Thomas Cranmer, the new Archbishop of Canterbury (secretly far more doctrinally alienated from the Catholic Church than Henry was) declared the Henry-Catherine marriage null and void and the Henry-Anne marriage, which had already secretly taken place, valid. Anne was crowned in Westminster Abbey; More was markedly absent. A daughter was born to Henry and Anne – the future Elizabeth I.

In the spring of 1534, an act was passed fixing the succession to the throne on the children of Henry and Anne and enjoining an oath to maintain that succession. Hot on the heels of that act came the Pope's declaration affirming the Henry-Catherine marriage. And hot on the heels of that came the summons to More to come to Cranmer's palace at Lambeth to take the oath. William Roper, Margaret's husband, describes More's departure from Chelsea on 13 April 1534:

> How, as was his custom in preparation for important business, he went to confession, Mass and Communion; how, against custom, he did not let his wife and children bring him to the boat and there get their farewell kiss but pulled the wicket after him and shut them all from him … and with me and our four servants there took his boat towards Lambeth … he suddenly rounded me in the ear and said 'son Roper, I thank the Lord the field is won'.

While willing to swear to the succession, More refused to take the oath. We do not know the wording of the oath, but we do know that it was to maintain 'the whole effects and contents of this present act' and that the act in its preamble repudiated the authority of the Pope in the realm. More rejected the oath because the oath rejected the Pope. Exercising his right to remain silent, he did not state his reason for rejection. The oath commissioners failed to persuade him otherwise; he was imprisoned in the Tower.

At the end of that year he was found guilty of misprision of treason and sentenced to life imprisonment and loss of goods. Around the same time the Act of Supremacy declared the king Supreme Head of the Church in his realm and the Act of Treasons made it treason and punishable by death to deny the king any of his titles. More's interrogators concentrated on the Supremacy but he refused to be drawn.

His Tower writings reveal a man focused on God and on his relationship with God. They include the classic *Dialogue of Comfort Against Tribulation* and the great prayer that begins: 'Give me thy grace, good Lord, to set the world at naught, to set my mind fast upon Thee and not to hang upon the blast of men's mouths'.

The Act of Supremacy claimed its first victims in the summer of 1535. Eight priests, six of them Carthusians, died at Tyburn; John Fisher, Bishop of Rochester, made cardinal while in prison, died on Tower Hill. On 1 July More went on trial in Westminster Hall on the charge of denying the Supremacy. The crux of the trial came with the evidence of Richard Rich, the solicitor-general. We do not know what he said exactly, but it seems certain that he alleged that More denied the Supremacy when he visited More in prison. More angrily rejected his evidence. The verdict was predictably 'guilty'.

Then at last More spoke out in love of 'Christ's Universal Catholic Church', as he liked to call it. His head-on attack with no punches pulled against the pretensions of the State is one of the great speeches in the history of Christian martyrdom.

The Act of Supremacy is directly repugnant to the law of God and of the Church. The supreme government of the Church or any part of it belongs to the see of Peter by a primacy granted by Christ to Saint Peter and his successors. The realm of England can no more make a law against the general law of the Church than London can make a law against an Act of Parliament for the whole realm. The king's claim violates *Magna Carta* and his coronation oath: 'For every bishop of yours [I have] above one hundred and for one Council or Parliament of yours ... I have all the Councils made these thousand years.' Thomas More was beheaded on Tower Hill on 6 July 1535.

Sweet Thames! run softly, softly run
from dawn to noon, to setting sun
from day to year, from youth to age
you've been my river, scene and stage
whereon I've acted out my play
until this hour, this Lambeth day
sweet Thames! run softly, softly run
praise God with me: the field is won.

Give us the grace, dear Lord, You gave to him
with mind set fast on You to fight and win.

HORIZONS EAST

FRANCIS

Francis Xavier's career began on 14 March 1540 in Rome when he was informed: 'You know that by order of the Pope two of us are to go to India. Bobadilla can't go because he's ill. The ambassador can't wait any longer. This is for you'. We have the exact words of Xavier's reply: *'Pues, sus! Heme aqui!'* – the Spanish equivalent of 'Great! Here I am!' Thus began one of the most remarkable mission careers in the history of the Church.

Francis Xavier was born in Castle Xavier in Navarre on 7 April 1506. His father was a doctor of law of prosperous peasant stock. His mother claimed descent from medieval nobility and part of her dowry was the small castle of Xavier. Francis was the youngest in the family.

The Xaviers combined sheep farming with aristocratic family pride and patriotic concern for their country, straddling the Pyrenees and threatened by the growing power of Spain. In 1516 Ferdinand of Aragon annexed Navarre to his kingdom of Aragon and Castile. In 1521 Francis' two brothers were in the thick of a French-assisted revolt against the Spaniards. One of them may have fired the shot at Pamplona that shattered the leg of a *caballero* named Iñigo Loyola.

Francis was reared in a tradition that took the Catholic faith seriously and unquestioningly. In 1525 he took the road to the University of Paris. He seems to have sat lightly enough to studies and he became one of the best high jumpers in the university. He is on record as saying that he was deterred from sexual sin by seeing its ravages in his master and fellow students.

He shared lodgings with a Savoyard named Pierre Favre. In 1529 they were joined by Iñigo Loyola, still limping from the Pamplona injury. With a conversion experience behind him, Iñigo was now devoted to gaining people for God. He won Pierre to his cause and angled patiently for Francis. The Xavier fish was elusive for a long time but at last took the bait. Years later, in another metaphor, Iñigo called him the lumpiest dough he had ever kneaded.

Francis was one of those who gathered at Montmarte on Assumption Day, 1534, and at a Mass celebrated by Favre (the only priest among them) he vowed poverty, chastity and, if possible, a pilgrimage to the Holy Land. Increased in numbers, the companions met in Venice in January 1537 to await a ship to Palestine. On 24 June some of them, including Francis, were ordained priests. The pilgrimage proved impossible, so in keeping with their vow they went to Rome to offer their services to the Pope.

One of the requests for their services came from John III of Portugal for the peoples in Asia under Portuguese control and influence. Two men were chosen but one fell ill. The matter was urgent – Iñigo thought of Francis. And so to 14 March 1540.

Francis did not arrive in Goa, the capital of Portugal's colonial empire in Asia, until mid-1542. This intermittent time consisted of months working in Lisbon (where the man who was to have been his missionary partner stayed at the king's request) and a year's voyage via the Cape of Good Hope. In Goa he became a legend of mercy, where he tried out simple methods of evangelising and soon realised that a major obstacle in the spreading of the faith was the lifestyle of some of the colonial officials.

Much of his work in India was along the southern coasts. He encountered the Paravas, poor pearl-fishers 'clamped to the sea', as he described them, who had been baptised but then left pastorless. He became 'clamped' to them, sharing their living conditions, always on the move along their burning sands. With the help of Paravan clerics (none of them priests) he taught them the rudiments of the faith in laboriously memorised Tamil. A second fishing people, the Macuas, came into his ken with sensational results: 'In one month I baptised more than ten thousand of them'. One of his Indian assistants had a similar 'catch' with a third fishing people, the Careas. Many of these were soon to be massacred by order of the fanatical Rajah of Jaffna.

After this martyrdom and prayer at the reputed tomb of the apostle Thomas at Mylepore (now a suburb of Madras), he decided to travel further east. So began the 'island phase' of his mission, mainly focused on those islanders who had been baptised without any 'follow-up'. Here he taught with more memorised catechesis, but this time in Malay.

At Malacca, on his way back to India, he met another instalment of providence in the shape of a fugitive from the law: Anjiro from Kagoshima in southern Japan, who had killed a man, probably accidentally, and escaped from Japan on a Portuguese ship. He was attracted to Francis as someone who could help him find peace of soul and must have been impressed by his missionary zeal. He provided him with a simplistic picture of Japan as a country that could be converted with comparative ease. On Assumption Day in 1549, the fifteenth anniversary of the Montemartre vows, Francis, two other Jesuits and Anjiro, by now a Catholic, arrived at Kagoshima.

As one Jesuit writer put it, with the Paravas Francis fished with a net, but in Japan he had to fish with a line. He struggled with the Japanese language, adapting to Japanese etiquette and living conditions, interminable hours of discussion, opposition from Buddhist priests (Francis called them 'bonzes'), as well as indifference and mockery. In Miyako (now Kyoto), the official capital of Japan, he realised that the *tenno*, often known as the *mikado*, was a pathetic shadow king without political power. The real rulers were the *daimyos*, the regional governors. It was by their grace and favour that the missionaries preached and ministered in Kagoshima and elsewhere.

Francis left Japan with hundreds of converts to be thankful for. He was impressed by their quality and felt that prospects for the Church were good and hoped to return. However, another country had come into his mind. He had noted how the Japanese had acknowledged their cultural dependence on China. They would ask: if what you say about the law of God and creation of the world is true, how come the Chinese do not know of it? But China was barred to foreigners.

On his way back to Goa he met a friend, Diogo Pereira, who showed him a letter he had received from one of the Portuguese imprisoned in Canton for illegal entry. The prisoner appealed to Pereira to get himself appointed envoy to China and secure their release. Francis thought: if Pereira was made envoy, could not he (Francis) be made his '*attaché*' and with him get permission from the Chinese emperor, 'the son of heaven', to preach the real kingdom of heaven in his empire?

And so it was done, but the official in charge of shipping at Malacca where their voyage was to begin, resenting Pereira's appointment, refused him permission to sail. Francis went on without him to Sancian Island off the south coast of China, a meeting place for Portuguese and Chinese merchants, and arranged with 'an honourable citizen of Canton' to smuggle him into China. He waited in vain and fell ill.

In the small hours of 3 December 1552, his faithful Chinese companion Antonio (no doubt a symbolic figure in his vision of a Christianised China) saw 'that he [Francis] was dying and put a lighted candle in his hand. Then with the name of Jesus on his lips he rendered his soul to his Creator and Lord with great repose and tranquillity.' And so Francis Xavier reached his last horizon in this life and sailed into another ocean of God.

Last night I dreamt that I was chasing sheep
across the valley, right across the sea
Ignatius kept on calling after me:
'Francis, you're the man to run and leap'.

I came ashore and walked on sands of fire
saw bonzes lining up with fishermen
and asking would I start baptising them
and I replied: 'The kingdom's not for hire'.

Demonic faces full of hate and threat
where are my friends of Xavier and Montmarte?
where are the fishers, children of my heart?
the faces closing in – I wake in sweat.

Where am I? Paris? India? Navarre?
Antonio comes – so faithful, one who cares
he holds my hands, in peace we say our prayers
and over China shines the morning star.

TO CHRIST HOMAGE

CAMILLUS

Two men in a friary garden in southern Italy: the superior of the Capuchins of Castello di Giovanni and the servant of the Capuchins of Manfredonia, come to collect a consignment of wine. Perhaps sensing that there was something 'special' about the tall, well-built young man with the scarred right foot, the superior delivered a one-to-one Spiritual exortation. On the way back to Manfredonia, the wine collector had a sudden insight into what his life had been. He fell on his knees and wept tears of repentance. It was Candlemas, 2 February 1575; Camillus de Lellis always remembered that day as the day of his 'moment of truth'.

He was born in Bucchianico in eastern Italy in 1550. Losing his mother while still a child, he grew up a harum-scarum and acquired a passion for gambling. He was named after his mother but took after his father who lived for soldiering, seeing service in various parts of Italy. Returning from a crusade against the Turks, the father died and the son developed a foot ulcer. The sight of a pair of Observantine Franciscans moved Camillus to vow to join their order, but his Franciscan uncle distrusted the impulse and declined to receive him.

Camillus next appeared first as a patient and then as a servant in the hospital of San Giacomo in Rome. As a servant he was a disaster, gaining the reputation of being a quarrelsome hothead, an obsessive card-player and a deserter from duty. His employers finally dismissed him. (Be it noted that this young man, so given to losing his temper and, through gambling, his belongings, was also given to keeping his chastity.)

He returned to soldiering again with a campaign against the Turks in Tunis; then back to Italy, getting to Manfredonia near Monte Gargano, the pilgrimage mountain dedicated to Saint Michael. He was quite destitute, reduced to begging. A local man got him a job with the Capuchin community. And so to the 'soul talk' in the garden and the experience on the road.

He became a Capuchin novice. But his foot wound reopened and his superiors reluctantly sent him away with the promise to readmit him if the ulcer healed. He returned to San Giacomo, first as a patient and then as a servant (a model one this time) and finally supervisor of the material goods of the hospital. Philip Neri, the 'Apostle of Rome', became his spiritual director. When the wound was almost healed, he returned to the novitiate, against Philip's advice: the wound would re-open, he said. And so it did, followed by yet another departure and another return to San Giacomo, this time to an appointment as hospital superintendent, which was followed by another application for admission to the Capuchins. Only when they, and the Observantines whom he had also approached, told him in writing why they were refusing him did he relinquish his 'impossible dream'. However, another dream was on the way.

Camillus became very aware of the defects of the hospital regime, including inadequate spiritual service and lack of trained staff. He made confession and communion more available to patients, prayed with those receiving communion, reminded staff of the religious side of their work and confronted delinquent staff to the point, if necessary, of dismissing them.

He formed a small group of like-minded men. They met daily in a room in the hospital for prayer, penance, reading and mutual encouragement before a large crucifix donated by friends. This crucifix became the symbol of their dedication to the sick. Despite difficulties with the hospital authorities, they maintained their identity and mission. Camillus' thoughts developed: for freedom of action and to attract recruits, should they leave San Giacomo and work from a house of their own, following a community rule of life and offering a whole-time and free service to the sick? And if a large part of the service was to be spiritual and sacramental, should not at least some of them be priests?

He himself was ordained priest in 1584. In 1586 Pope Sixtus V approved 'the Company of the Ministers of the Sick' whose members, though not taking public vows, lived in poverty, celibacy and obedience and devoted themselves to the sick. In that year the Company made their home at the church of Saint Mary

Magdalene. The Maddalena became and still is the headquarters of the Camillians and the famous crucifix is still honoured there. In 1591 the Company climbed the canonical ladder to become an Order.

The rules he wrote for the Company surely reflect his experience of illness in himself and in others, including those he had fought with and against in his pre-conversion days. The sick are to be tended with 'motherly love'. The inscription he ordered to be put over a hospital door sums up his thoughts: 'To Christ, God and man, sick in the person of the poor, homage and love'. His companions treasured memories of his tenderness towards the sick: warming their feet, bathing them in tepid water and cooking 'specials' for them (he was an excellent cook). They might have doubted his prudence in government on occasion (as when they resisted him regarding his plan for what he called 'complete service' of the sick, which they considered too demanding) but they never doubted his sanctity.

His favourite workplace was the Santo Spirito hospital in Rome; he called it his 'garden' in which he found happiness. And he must have found happiness too in seeing his men wearing the distinctive Camillian cross and becoming an established part of the hospital scene in Italy. In drawing up rules for a comprehensive service for soldiers campaigning in Croatia and Hungary (a foreshadowing of the modern Red Cross/Diamond) he must surely have recalled his own soldiering and prayed for his former comrades and enemies-in-arms.

He resigned office in 1607, which left him more time for direct care of the sick. The ulcer which had been so providential in his life proved a 'permanent fixture' and indeed became worse – he called it and his other ailments his 'five mercies'. But his strong body finally broke down and he died at the Maddalena on 14 July 1614.

Paul had his road experience, so had I
Candlemas feast in fifteen seventy-five
beneath Saint Michael's sky
but not a light like Simeon's – pure, serene
rather a flash to make me all alive
to seek another scene
and find in battle-field and street and ward
in sick and poor my suffering Saviour-Lord.

BY SLANEY AND LIFFEY

THE MARTYRS OF WEXFORD AND DUBLIN

Many Irish people died for the Catholic faith in the sixteenth and seventeenth centuries. In 1992 Pope John Paul II beatified almost twenty of them from the period 1579 to 1654. A second group of about forty is currently being considered for beatification. Most of those already beatified died in Wexford and Dublin, but the Dublin proto-martyr is not among them. John Travers is still canonically ranked as 'Venerable'. He was a graduate in two degrees of the University of Oxford and Chancellor of Saint Patrick's Cathedral, Dublin. He was executed in the 1530s for refusing to acknowledge the supremacy of Henry VIII in Church matters. He has a special place in the history of the Church in Dublin and deserves to be remembered by Dublin Catholics. Think of him when you pass by or visit Saint Patrick's.

In 1570 Pope Pius V excommunicated Elizabeth Tudor, declared her deposed and her subjects released from allegiance to her. The idea of a military crusade to restore Catholicism in England (to culminate in the Spanish Armada) developed. The Catholic response to the Protestant challenge was under way in continental Europe and this filtered into Ireland. In 1579 James Fitzmaurice Fitzgerald, cousin of the Earl of Desmond, arrived in Kerry with the Pope's legate and blessing and a small force and proclaimed a crusade against Elizabeth. He died in action shortly afterwards but his rising developed with the Earl himself as its leader.

In Leinster, James FitzEustace, Viscount Baltinglass, who like Fitzmaurice had returned from the continent with a strengthened faith, denounced the queen and went into rebellion. But his rising failed and he came to Wexford with his Jesuit friend Robert Rochford, hoping to escape from that port. A baker, Matthew Lambert, and some sailors (it seems that there were five: Robert Meyler, Edward Cheevers, Patrick Cavanagh/Canavan; one account has John O'Lahy instead of Cavanagh; the names of one or two are unknown) faced trial for befriending them.

Lambert, speaking, it seems, for all of them, said that he was loyal to the queen, that he did not understand the pope versus queen dilemma and that he believed in the faith of his mother, the Holy Catholic Church. These brave working-class laymen of simple faith were found guilty of treason and barbarously executed in July 1581.

In 1583 Dermot Ó Hurley, appointed Archbishop of Cashel after a long academic life, arrived in Ireland. A guest of the Flemings of Slane Castle, County Meath, he aroused the suspicions of another guest who reported him to the lords justices, who were in charge of the English administration in Ireland. They ordered the Slane baron to produce the archbishop, 'or else'. A frightened Fleming induced him to come to Dublin where he was imprisoned in Dublin Castle.

He denied involvement in 'treasons' and remained, according to the justices, obstinate and evasive, and on instructions from London they had him tortured: his legs were thrust into boots filled with oil and held to a fire. Charles MacMorris Lea, a Jesuit with medical skill, tended his wounds. Elizabeth forbade any more torture and left it to the justices to opt either for trial by jury or trial by martial law. They chose the latter and the verdict was, of course, guilty.

He was hanged in the early morning of Saturday, 20 June 1584 in Hoggen Green, a semi-rural area on the south side of the Liffey. Unexpectedly, the execution was witnessed by the public in the form of some citizens come to engage in their weekend archery. These surprised men found themselves being told by a waistcoated man under guard that he was being put to death for his ministry and profession of the Catholic faith. The traditional site of his grave is Saint Kevin's Park near Saint Patrick's Cathedral.

Around the same time, an indomitable woman died in prison in Dublin for the Catholic faith: Margaret (Bermingham) Ball. Her own family and that of her husband, a wealthy Dublin merchant, were devout Catholics, but one family member turned out to be a deep disappointment in their eyes: her son Walter became a Protestant. Her house was a centre of Catholic doctrine, to her own household and through her servants to other households, and also a shelter for priests – on one occasion she was marched off to prison because a priest was caught celebrating Mass there. Released through 'good offices', she resumed her apostolate.

Walter became Mayor of Dublin and it was during his term of office, and at least with his connivance, that she was imprisoned again. This time there was no release. She is Dublin's counterpart to London's Anne Line and York's Margaret Clitherow.

In 1603 the most formidable struggle to date against English rule in Ireland came to an end with the surrender of its leader, Hugh O'Neill. James VI of Scotland, the son of Mary Queen of Scots, whom Catholics considered a martyr, became James I of England and Ireland. Much to the Catholics' disappointment, he proved strongly anti-Catholic (the Gunpowder Plot was doubtless a factor in this) and the Act of the Uniformity that made attendance at Protestant worship legally compulsory was revived; Catholic clergy in general and Jesuits in particular were to be expelled from Ireland.

On 28 January 1612, as part of a plan to discredit Catholic bishops for alleged non-religious offences and to undermine Catholic morale, Conor Ó Devany, Bishop of Down and Connor, and Patrick Ó Loughran, a priest who had once been a chaplain in Hugh O'Neill's household, (both already in prison) were put on trial for treason. The verdict was guilty and the horrific executions of hanging, drawing and quartering took place on 1 February in the Oxmantown area on the north side of the Liffey. The crowd surrounding the gallows was immense. The executions, planned to intimidate Catholics, became an occasion of a public and collective profession of faith. Ó Devany and Ó Loughran are the most publicly, most immediately acclaimed martyrs in the history of Dublin. The Oxmantown scene brings to mind the Carthage scene of Cyprian's death thirteen and a half centuries earlier.

Francis Taylor came from Swords, County Dublin, of a family prominent in the life of the city. Sheriff, treasurer and mayor were among the posts he held. A parliament in which the Dublin Castle administration hoped Catholic influence would be at least minimised and anti-Catholic measures facilitated was due to meet in 1613. Francis Taylor was one of the two Catholics who strongly claimed against two Protestants to be the validly elected MPs.

It was not long before he found himself in prison, a victim of the anti-Catholic campaign of the administration, still smarting from their propaganda failure in the Ó Devany and Ó Loughran event, and probably determined to show their clout by 'getting' the city's leading Catholic. It seems certain that he was sentenced by the Court of Castle Chamber. This court could bypass statute law and ordinary legal procedures and had wide punitive powers. It was the counterpart of the Court of Star Chamber, an instrument of State tyranny in England.

For several years until his death this man (Dublin's counterpart to London's Thomas More), already elderly by the standard of his time, who had been a respected figure of the city establishment and had lived in comfortable circumstances, endured the hardships of imprisonment. He died on 29/30 January 1621. A few weeks previously he had made his will, remembering along with his family matters to leave something for 'poor people in way of devotion for my soul's health'.

In 1641 Ulster exploded in insurrection. The northern Irish, dispossessed by the plantation of thirty years previous, rose against the planters and soon had most of the province under their control, but not without murder and arson.

The rising spread to Leinster. The insurgents seized Naas, twenty miles from Dublin. Terrified Protestants found a protector in the prior of the Dominican community: Peter Higgins. The Marquis of Ormond, commander of the royal forces, recaptured the town. He took the prior under his protection, refused custody of him to Charles Coote, the very anti-Catholic governor of Dublin and hunter of priests, promised him justice and gave him a safe conduct to Dublin.

A fellow Dominican ministered to him in prison. Protestants affirmed his goodness to them. It is very likely that there was no formal trial. He died by hanging on 23 March 1642. There can hardly be any doubt that Coote was the prime mover in his death. Ormond had underestimated the ruthless determination of 'the hunter of priests'.

On the scaffold he affirmed his innocence of crime and his loyalty to the Catholic faith and to his religious profession. In his 'ecumenism' he was something of a prophet. This member of the Order of Preachers preached his best sermon by the way he died.

Slaney and Liffey meeting the tide
greeting the eastern sea
here's where they died
clergy and laity.

Baker, sailors, widow, ex-mayor
bishops, priests: one Love to share.

Slaney and Liffey meeting the foam
ending their seaward race
here they came home
began to love face to face.

ACROSS THE SEA

IRISH MARTYRS IN ENGLAND AND WALES

The Church in England and Wales has a long honour roll of martyrs from the sixteenth and seventeenth centuries: over three hundred in all with about two hundred canonised or beatified. Four of those beatified were Irish; two had Irish connections.

John Roche/Neale was an Irish boatman in London. He and Margaret Ward (now canonised) helped a priest, William Watson, to escape from prison. Under an extension of the infamous anti-priest act of 1585 (see below) this was enough for them to be condemned as traitors. They were barbarously executed at Tyburn in 1588.

A woman and a half, that Margaret Ward
a real battling soldier of the Lord
full of spirit, daring everything
(her name means one of those sought-after gems).

A nice job for a boatman, you could say
helping a priest escape: he got away
we didn't and tomorrow we will swing
embarking on a river not the Thames.

John Cornelius was a Cornishman, born in Bodmin of Irish parents. After studies in Oxford and on the continent and priestly ordination, he returned to the West Country and joined the Jesuits. He was charged under the act of 1585, which declared it high treason for a native-born subject of the Crown after priestly ordination abroad to return and minister in the realm without surrendering himself to the authorities within forty-eight hours of arrival.

He was executed at Dorchester in 1594. With him died three 'serving men' of his condemned (like Margaret Ward and John Roche) under an extension of the act for assisting or harbouring a priest. Two of these were Irish: John Carey and Patrick Salmon.

West Country this: my roots more western still
I look my last on Cornish towns
on Devon orchards, Dorset downs
and find in Dorchester my Calvary hill.

We served his Mass, we ran his messages
kept everything ship-shape, no fuss
half-Irish, he was dear to us
and now in death with him we enter bliss.

Ralph Corby/Corbington (1598–1644) spent his first years in the Maynooth area of County Kildare where his father was employed by the Countess of Kildare. When he was still a little boy the family moved to his father's native County Durham. Prolonged anti-Catholic harassment forced them to emigrate to Saint Omer in Flanders. After studies in Spain Ralph was ordained priest, joined the Jesuits and was assigned to their English mission.

For several years this gentle man of frail health and, according to himself, 'few talents' was (to quote a confrere) 'in his paradise with the poor Catholics at Durham and the villages.' Paradise ended when Puritan raiders, fresh from their victory at Marston Moor in the English civil war, burst into the house where he was saying Mass. He and another priest, John Duckett, were brought to London. As Irish-born he asked, in vain of course, for a trial in Ireland. They were found guilty under the 1585 act and executed at Tyburn on 7 September 1644.

Maynooth, Ryewater, Liffeyland, Kildare
Derwent, Villadolid and Saint Omer
Durham villages and Tyburn tree
And Raphael comes to heal you utterly.

Charles Meehan/Mihan, an Irish Franciscan, suffered the same fate. Because of a flare-up of persecution in the 1670s, he left Ireland and spent a few years in Franciscan communities on the continent. The ship bringing him back to Ireland was driven on to the Welsh coast. He was arrested at Denbigh and executed at Ruthin on 12 August 1679.

This was the time of the horrific anti-Catholic hysteria whipped up by Titus Oates and his associates with their reports of a Popish-Jesuit plot to assassinate the king and ensure a Catholic dynasty. Some victims of the hysteria (like Oliver Plunkett, Archbishop of Armagh) were barbarously executed as conspirators. Others (like Peter Talbot, Archbishop of Dublin) died in prison. Others again were put to death not as plotters, but as traitorous transgressors of the 1585 anti-priest act. Charles Meehan was one of these.

Ship goes astray
Wales, not Ireland, hoves in sight
Denbigh, Ruthin: into light
God knows the way.

AMERICAN CAMEOS

FROM LAS CASAS TO SERRA

Bartolomé de Las Casas (1474–1566), whose father had sailed with Columbus, combined, both before and after becoming a Dominican, missionary zeal and loyalty to the Spanish Crown with a passionate defence of Indians exploited by unscrupulous colonists. A tireless writer, he fought for their rights into his old age, persuading the Crown to enact the 'New Laws' that, despite opposition, did something to revise colonial policy and protect the Indians. He can to some extent be considered a forerunner of the 'faith and justice' apostolate favoured by many modern missionaries.

Joseph de Anchieta (1534–1597) from Tenerife, Canary Islands, spent nearly all his Jesuit life in Brazil preaching the gospel, supervising the mission and improving the quality of life of the people. Because of his religious dedication he is known as 'the Apostle of Brazil'. Because of his writings both in Portuguese and in the regional Tupi he is considered the founder of Brazilian literature. This great man in the history of Brazil had the town of his death and burial named after him.

Roch Gonzalez (1576–1628), a Paraguayan and already a priest when he joined the Jesuits, had good rapport with the indigenous Indians, defending them against oppressive colonists, gathering them into Jesuit settlements ('reductions') and forming them in the faith. In all this he was helped by two Spanish Jesuits: Alfonso Rodriguez and John del Castillo. On 15 November 1628 a witch doctor, fanatically resentful of their influence with the Indians, murdered Roch and Alfonso and two days later murdered John.

In the 1640s six priests of the Society of Jesus and two lay assistants, all French, working on the mission to the Huron Indians suffered martyrdom. Three of them died at what is now Auriesville in New

York State: Isaac Jogues and the two laymen, René Goupil and Jean La Lande. Five of them died in the western Great Lakes region in what was then New France and is now Canada: Antoine Daniel, Jean de Brébeuf, Gabriel Lalemant, Charles Garnier and Noel Chabanel. Two of the deaths were perpetrated by Mohawks, five by Iroquios and one (that of Chabanel) by a Huron apostate. There are two much frequented sanctuaries dedicated to these heroic men: one at Auriesville in honour of three of them; and the other at Midland, Ontario in honour of five. It is consoling to note that some twenty to twenty-five years after the Great Lakes martyrdoms the Iroquios agreed to accept Jesuit missionaries.

Influenced by Alfonso Rodriguez, the saintly doorkeeper of the Jesuit college in Palma, Majorca, Pedro Claver (1580–1654) decided to be a missionary in America. Ordained priest at Cartagena, Colombia, he dedicated himself to the service of those brought there as slaves from Africa, an immense and seemingly endless 'congregation', seeing himself as the 'permanent slave of the slaves: *aethiopum semper servus*' (or so he gave his 'job description' when he signed his final vows). In this commitment he was influenced by his colleague Alonso de Sandoval, who was angrily and articulately concerned about those children of Africa, torn from their homes, as Claver put it, 'along the rivers of Africa' and facing an alien world. Pedro Claver became a legend of 'hands-on' compassion and love to those victims of an evil and dehumanising commerce. In his old age he was a victim of paralysis and maltreatment by a so-called nurse. Not surprisingly, he is the patron saint of missions to black peoples.

Kateri (Katharine) Tekakwitha (c. 1656–1680), an Indian girl, the 'Lily of the Mohawks' as she came to be called, lived for nearly all her life in what is now Auriesville in the State of New York. Her mother was a Christian and her father a pagan Mohawk chief. She was baptised at Easter 1676. To escape from a hostile pagan environment she trekked nearly two hundred miles to a Christian village near Montreal. There she led an austere and pain-ridden life. She dedicated herself to Christ by a vow of celibacy and was intently devoted to the Blessed Eucharist. After her death she became the unofficial heavenly patron of the village community.

Junipero Serra (1713–1784) from Majorca worked for many years in Mexico and then moved to Lower California as president/supervisor of the Franciscan mission enterprise there. His remit later extended to Upper California in tandem with Spanish colonial advance. He founded several missions, some of them in what is now the San Francisco conurbation. In a broad sense he can be considered one of the founders of the famous city. He was devoted to his Indians and introduced them not only to the gospel, but to agriculture as well (he was the son of a farmer). Like Las Casas and the aforementioned Paraguayan trio, he defended them against oppression: somewhere in Spanish colonial archives is the memorial he sent to the Viceroy in Mexico City about the treatment of His Catholic Majesty's Indian subjects.

This great apostle of California died and was interred at his headquarters, the mission of San Carlos, Monterey-Carmel. There is a statue of him in the Hall of Fame in Washington.

Another world, a double continent
mighty rivers, forests, mountain peaks
sun, wind, colour, surely all this speaks
of God Creator – but they're chosen, sent
with something more to say.

They bring the Word, the sacramental Christ
following him, they heal, defend the poor
they pray, they work, they hope, they fear, endure
some share his very death, die sacrificed
the harvest's on the way.

WOMEN AGAINST THE LAW

NANO AND TERESA

Nano

Around 1718, Garret and Ann Nagle of Ballygriffin, Mallow, County Cork had their first child, whom they christened Honora and pet-named Nano. It was the time of the anti-Catholic penal laws which were to be the backdrop of the drama of her life. The second half of her life was to be a crusade to counter these laws, insofar as they were an attack on Catholic schooling.

One of those laws, aimed at reducing the wealth and social status of Catholic landowners, was the Gavelkind Act, whereby Catholic-owned land had to be 'gavelled' (divided) rather than passed on to one heir. Under this law, Nano's father had inherited only part of his father's estate. As she grew up, Nano became aware of members of her own social class conforming at least externally to the established Church to protect their property, of only 'registered' priests being legally allowed to minister to their people, of the need for discretion in religious practice, of cautiously expressed regrets for the defeat of the House of Stuart and the victory of the Houses of Orange and Hanover.

It is likely enough that she was a boarder at the Irish Benedictine convent in Ypres in Flanders; many children of her social class received a continental 'finishing' despite the legal ban on education abroad for Catholics. For some years she enjoyed life in Paris in the more affluent part of its large post-Treaty of Limerick Irish colony. After the death of her father around 1746, she lived with her mother in Dublin. After her mother's death in 1748 she returned to Ballygriffin. Her sister Ann also died shortly afterwards.

A new, more mature Nano began to appear. It seems that Ann's death and the memory of her 'uncommon piety' affected her deeply, and that she became acutely aware of the widespread superstition among the Irish poor, corrosive of their Catholic faith and human dignity; she became aware that behind this were the related spectres of the penal code in regard to education and the educational efforts of the politico-religious establishment, which were aimed at conversion to the established Church.

What could she do in all this? In a sort of trauma of perceived helplessness she fled to France with the idea of becoming a cloistered nun. A Jesuit counsellor told her that her vocation was to poor Irish children. So back to Ireland and to Cork city, to stake her claim and fly her flag.

She began with thirty girls in Cove Lane and altogether founded seven schools in the city: five for girls, two for boys. Her special work was teaching catechism and preparing the children for the sacraments. She enjoyed giving religious instruction. 'I often think my schools will never bring me to heaven,' she wrote with a touch of humour, 'as I only take delight and pleasure in them.' Did she also secretly enjoy with a stir of Nagle family feeling (her father had Jacobite sympathies and her grand-uncle had ranked high in the short-lived administration of James II) her illegal success in matters religious at the expense of the Williamite-Hanoverian Ascendancy?

Along with her teaching (of adults as well as of children) she managed the schools, paid the teachers, when necessary begged, visited the poor and sick and founded a hostel for elderly women. In a prophetic outreach she organised past pupils of the boys' schools who joined the merchant navy to be apostles of the faith in the West Indies among the Irish there. Underpinning and permeating all this was continual prayer and penance. The Paris socialite had come a long way.

Her chief supporter in money matters was her uncle, Joseph. Other relatives helped too, including her cousin, the political philosopher Edmund Burke, who famously described and denounced the penal laws and parliamentarily helped to ease them.

To ensure continuity for her work, Nano was anxious to get the assistance of a religious order. She made an agreement with some Paris Ursulines whereby they would train aspirants she sent them for the planned Ursuline community in Cork. The Ursulines did come, but their rule of enclosure prevented them from being the 'walking nuns' that she had envisaged – they were of help in only one school.

This dedicated woman proceeded to found a congregation of unenclosed 'walking nuns'; in 1778 with three companions she took first vows in the Sisters of Charitable Instruction of the Sacred Heart. (Perhaps the mention of the Sacred Heart is an echo from the Benedictine convent in Ypres, which was a centre of the devotion.) After her death the congregation was re-named the Sisters of the Presentation of the Blessed Virgin Mary.

She died on 26 April 1784. In her fulfilment of God's law of love for the little ones of this world she had quietly defied unjust man-made law. She had pioneered a remarkable revival of consecrated life in Ireland. She had lived up to the Nagle mottos: 'Not words but deeds'.

Teresa

Nano had a contemporary kindred spirit in Dublin: Teresa Mulally. She was born in 1728, the only child of Daniel and Elizabeth Mulally. Her father ran a provisions business. She spent virtually all her life in Oxmantown, the historic originally Norse area north of the Liffey, earning a modest living as a milliner.

Like Nano, Teresa was concerned about the daughters of the poor. In 1766 she rented a space at the top of a house near Mary's Lane chapel, where she attended Mass. With the Ascendancy power centres close by in Dublin Castle and College Green, the milliner began her challenge to their anti-Catholic laws concerning education. Supporting her were dedicated teachers, Miss Clinch and Miss Corballis, and the Jesuit Father Philip Mulcaile, newly come from France and working at Saint Michan's in Mary's Lane.

The girls learned arithmetic, reading, spelling, needlework and other skills. They learned their catechism and prayers and attended Mass daily. After Sunday Mass there was an instruction. In 1771 a small boarding school was opened.

In 1782 Gardiner's second Catholic Relief Act included the legislation of Catholic schools under certain conditions. Legal at last, Teresa became exempt from window tax and, supported by the rector and vestry of the Church of Ireland Saint Michan's (a sign of more tolerant times), from being taxed for the benefit of the Protestant parish.

In 1787 she bought a disused factory at George's Hill and, while a few streets away the splendid Four Courts of Cooley and Gandon took shape, she built her rather less imposing convent and school. This was to prepare for the long hoped-for coming of Nano's sisters to continue her work. The sisters finally arrived in 1794 to begin a Presentation presence, which still endures.

Not becoming a sister herself, she lived in the orphanage beside the convent, taking care of the material needs of the establishment and being a mother figure to its younger members. This remarkable woman, who combined deep love of God and the poor with business acumen, died on 3 February 1803. Her remains rest in the former chapel crypt, along with those of her faithful friend Philip Mulcaile.

Nearby are three special mementoes of her: the crucifix, reputedly used by Saint Francis Xavier, that Father Mulcaile brought from France and that she reverenced so often; the Calvary rockery of stones from the penal-day Saint Michan's where she attended Mass; and the holy water font (still in use in the present Saint Michan's) in which she dipped her hand to bless herself, ensuring that her beloved children blessed themselves too.

> *Tale of two cities: Cove Lane, George's Hill*
> *Nano, Teresa: two women one in will*
> *to fly a flag, to challenge, make a fight*
> *for children of the poor, defend their right*
> *to learn and know and grow in dignity*
> *as children of the Lord, enriched and free.*

> *Lee and Liffey: still they flow and sing*
> *Nano, Teresa: worth remembering*
> *you planted, others harvested the fruit*
> *you flew a flag: we thank you, we salute.*

LAYMAN IN LOVE

FRÉDÉRIC

In 1833, some students of the University of Paris were debating the social teaching of the gospel. An anti-Catholic speaker challenged the Catholic students: 'What is your Church doing now? What is she doing for the poor of Paris? Show us your works and we will believe you'. One of the students thus challenged was Frédéric Ozanam.

He was born in Milan, at that time under French control, on 23 April 1813. When French rule collapsed in Italy the Ozanams returned to their native Lyons. They traced their line to Samuel Hozannam, a seventh-century convert Jew whose Lyons roots went back to the first century before Christ.

His father was a doctor who cared for his patients often beyond the call of duty and without fee and with his wife often helping him. This remembered goodness of his parents may well have been a motive in his own decision years later to serve the poor.

Halfway through his teenage years, Frédéric had a year-long crisis of faith. Helped by his teacher Abbé Noirot, he emerged from this crisis a more convinced Christian, with the aim of becoming an informed exponent and defender of the faith. Two or three years later he produced his first work as a Christian apologist, a critique of the teaching of the 'messianic' social philosopher Saint-Simon. Parisian intellectuals sat up and took note of this new young voice.

He became a student of law at the University of Paris. He made the acquaintance of leaders of the post-Revolution Catholic revival including Chateaubrand and Montalambert (writers and politicians), Lacordaire (former ex-Catholic, then diocesan priest, later a Dominican and most remembered as the great Notre Dame preacher and re-founder of the Dominicans in France) and Ampére (distinguished mathematician and physicist). After his graduation he was called to the bar in Lyons.

Auguste Le Taillandier, a student friend of Frédéric, suggested that the response to the 'show us your works' challenge should be their own 'hands-on' service of the poor. This was accepted and in due course the Conference of Charity had its first meeting of Frédéric and five other students, with their philosophy professor and mentor Emmanuel Bailly presiding.

Their guide to those in need was Rosalie Rendu, who had worked among the poor of Paris for many years. She can be considered one of the founders of their enterprise. She was of the Daughters of Charity, the congregation founded by Louise de Marillac and Vincent de Paul. Conscious of her services and of her Vincentian background, the conferenciers re-named themselves the Society of Saint Vincent de Paul, with him as their patron saint.

Essentially and, one might say, prophetically a lay organisation, the Society spread, becoming international in the 1840s. Shortly after Frédéric's death in 1853 it had over one thousand five hundred centres in Europe, Africa, Asia Minor and North America. Its first Irish centre was established in Halston Street parish (Saint Michan's) in Dublin in 1844, in what had been Teresa Mulally territory in the preceding century.

Much of the inspiration for all of this came from Frédéric. He stressed the dignity of the poor and saw the Society's work for them, whether they were Catholics or not, as part of a gospel-based social reform: 'The poor person is a unique person of God's fashioning with an inalienable right to respect. You must not be content with tiding the poor over the poverty crisis. You must study their condition and the injustices which brought about such poverty, with the aim of a long-term improvement'.

His apostolate among the poor was in tandem with his academic career, mostly in Paris: doctorates in law and literature; professor of commercial law in Lyons; lecturer and then professor of foreign literature in Paris.

At one point he thought of being a priest and religious, but on the advice of Abbé Noirot decided against it. In 1841 he married the daughter of the president of the Lyons Academy. They had one child, Marie, whom he adored. He also adored his wife Emilie and romantically arranged that on the twenty-third of every month she would receive a bouquet of flowers.

With friends he founded *L'Ere Nouvelle* ('The New Era'), a newspaper with a Catholic perspective. (It can be seen as a precursor of the famous *La Croix* ('The Cross'), founded by Vincent de Paul Bailly, Emmanuel's son.) He encouraged Catholics to take part in democratic politics. In this he foreshadowed the work of leaders like Sturzo, de Gasperi, Schumann and Adenauer in the following century. He insisted that 'it is truth which will always rise to judge political systems'. In one section of his commercial law course he anticipated the social teaching of Pope Leo XIII in his great encyclical, *Rerum Novarum* (1891), was on the condition of workers and related issues. Perhaps the Lyons script was one of Leo's sources.

From his mid-thirties, Frédéric's health, which had never been that good, was in definite decline. In 1853, while in Italy, he realised that he was near death. He wanted to die in Paris; he got as far as Marseilles, where he died on 8 September. Two weeks before, on 23 August, Emilie had received her flowers.

Layman in love: so many hours
given to truth in deed and word
to the poor the gospel one-to-one
seeing in them God's, Mary's Son
and every day the twenty-third
saying his love in a spray of flowers.

WORDS AND MUSIC

FROM JOHN OF THE CROSS TO CÉSAR FRANCK

John of the Cross (Juan de Yepes y Alvarez, 1542–1591) came of a silk-weaving family in Fontiveros in central Spain. He is one of the glories of the Carmelite tradition and one of the most renowned mystics in the history of the Church. His writings (many of them poems) are important in the history and theology of Christian mysticism. The poems are treasures of Spanish literature. He no doubt set them to chords, being a guitarist.

He worked with Teresa of Avila, whom he spiritually directed, to establish a more prayerful and more austere lifestyle in the Order. Some friars, in an effort to get him to renounce the work of reform, imprisoned him in appalling conditions. During this time he composed nearly all the poems of *The Spiritual Canticle*. They were in his mind at first, then, by courtesy of a benign jailer, in written form. Finally, he managed to escape back to the open air where he loved to pray, especially at night. Back too, one hopes, to his guitar.

His best-known words are: 'When the evening of this life comes, we shall be judged on love'. *The Spiritual Canticle* stanzas have a special value. He called them 'utterances of love arising from mystical understanding' – words of surrender to the All-beautiful, the All-desired. Here is a version of some of these 'utterances', composed almost certainly in a prison cell in Toledo:

> Day by day in rain and sun/on mountains, by the sea/I will seek my Promised One/seek him utterly/All I find is from his hand/meadows lush in grass/trees and flowers, a lovely land/did you see him pass?/He was here, my Love in haste/looked at them and shone/left them beautiful, engraced/loved them and was gone/gentle water, crystal spring/give this gift to me/make your face a mirroring/of eyes I long to see.
> *(English composition by Stephen Redmond SJ)*

Robert Southwell (1561–1595) came of Norfolk gentry. He became a Jesuit and a priest and joined the dangerous English mission in 1584. For him writing was a tool of apostolate, but it was also part of the great literary movement of the time whose chief glory was Shakespeare; and indeed he made an important contribution to English recusant literature. His *The Burning Babe*, perhaps the best known of his poems, is a vision piece, rather like the *aislingí* of penal-day Irish poets.

He was befriended by Anne, Countess of Arundel, whose husband, Philip Howard, a convert to Catholicism, was in prison and was to die there. Robert wrote him letters of encouragement and spiritual direction. An expansion of the letters became *The Letter of Comfort*, a counterpart of More's *Dialogue of Comfort Against Tribulation*. This poet, who was surely close to the Heart of Christ, endured many sessions of torture and was hanged, drawn and quartered at Tyburn under the infamous anti-priest act of 1585.

George Herbert (1593–1633), Welsh aristocrat and loyal Anglican, and enjoying the patronage of James I, had a more comfortable life than Southwell's, but had a similar poetic gift. In later life he felt drawn to a more spiritual form of life and was ordained into the Anglican ministry and became parson of a rural parish in Wiltshire. He said his prayers, tended his parish and wrote his poetry.

He wrote only religious verse (in this perhaps influenced by Southwell). It was of a high standard: 'my God must have my best'. He composed *The Temple*, a remarkable collection of one hundred and sixty poems on Christian life, a sort of prolonged meditation on Saint Paul's text in his first letter to the Christians of Corinth about God dwelling in those in grace. It ends with an exquisite poem, simply titled 'Love' – Christ welcoming the repentant sinner.

The Sunday before he died, Herbert rose from his sickbed and praised God on lute and viola in these lines: 'My God, my God/my music shall find thee/and every string/shall have its attribute to sing'. A moving example of a final testament of worship in words and music.

Tadhg Gaelach O'Súilleabháin (c. 1715–1795) was a poet of the 'hidden Ireland', of a majority culture discriminated against in religion, politics, education and social and economic status – one of those who helped to keep alive in that culture the tradition of poetry in Irish. It is very likely that he came from the Cork-Limerick borderland. He spent his last thirty years in County Waterford. It is widely accepted that he was a member of the Confraternity of the Sacred Heart, established in Dungarvan by Edward Lisward of the Society of Jesus, who was parish priest there in the mid-eighteenth century. O'Súilleabháin is said to have died in the 'Big Chapel' in Waterford City, saying his prayers.

He has a claim to be considered the greatest religious poet in modern Irish. Our Lady is lyrically presented, his favourite name for her being '*réiltean*': star, fair lady. The two poems about '*An Paidrín Páirteach*' ('The Rosary Together') may well echo a confraternity practice. *Gile mo Chroí* ('Radiance of My Heart'), the most celebrated poem in Irish in honour of the Sacred Heart, of which he is the generally accepted author, has the marks of a personalised confraternity spirituality. Here is a translation of the beginning and conclusion of this masterpiece:

> Dear Lord, your Heart is the radiance of my own/my heart delights that yours is so near to me/clearly your Heart keeps loving me utterly/so make your Heart a shield for my heart deep down/You came from heaven, you walked on human shore/in mystery you suffered for all our sin/guiding in love the lance that allowed us in/and made your Heart our dwelling forevermore.
> *(Translation by Stephen Redmond SJ)*

During the years when Tadhg Gaelach was saying his Rosary in Waterford, another 'Rosary man' was making music in central Europe. It is said that Franz Joseph Haydn (1732–1806) would 'tell the beads' between stints of composing. He was a kindly and affable man; his pupils in the aristocratic Esterhazy establishment affectionately called him 'Papa'. He can be considered the 'father figure' in the famous trio of himself, Mozart and Beethoven.

There were complaints that some of his music for Mass was too lighthearted for church use. He famously replied: 'When I think of the Lord my heart is so joyfull that the notes come running of themselves. God gave me a joyful heart, so he may forgive me for serving him joyfully'.

This joy found special expression in his great oratorio *The Creation*, a celebration of nature and of the gifts of God, with heart-lifting choruses like 'Let there be Light' and 'The Heavens are telling the Glory of God'. His last public appearance was at a gala performance of it, with Beethoven publicly acknowledging his musical debt to Haydn.

When the French, at war with Austria, occupied Vienna in 1806, Napoleon placed a guard of honour at the composer's house. He died on 31 May. French and Austrians united in respect at his funeral. It was a good send off for Papa Haydn.

Gerard Manley Hopkins (1844–1889) came of a well-off, devoutly Anglican family. While at Oxford he was received into the Catholic Church by John Henry Newman. Shortly after graduation he joined the Society of Jesus and was ordained a priest in 1877. His last posting was to University College Dublin where he taught classics.

He wrote a new kind of lyric poetry. The philosophy of Duns Scotus with its emphasis on individual reality, Saint Ignatius' presentation of Christ as a king asking for generous service, his devotion to the Sacred Heart, the subtlety of natural things, his own sensitive personality – he expressed such themes and influences in verse of what he called 'sprung rhythm' or 'imitative rhythm'. It was a system related to the rhythms of music in keeping with the subject matter (he was a pianist and violinist and something of a minor composer). It could be called writing and speaking poetry with music in mind.

In a way reminiscent of John of the Cross, he spoke (or sang) of 'the dearest freshest deep down things', of 'the air we breathe' as a reminder of Our Lady, of 'dappled things', of a world 'charged with the grandeur of God'. The last words of this poet whose verse was akin to music were luminous and lyrical: 'I am so happy'.

John Henry Newman (1801–1890) was an Anglican for the first half of his life and a Catholic for the second, and had a profound influence on both communions. He was a leading light in the Oxford Movement, which challenged the Anglican establishment with a Catholicising interpretation of Anglican doctrine. He became a Catholic in 1845 and subsequently an Oratorian and a cardinal. In his emphasis on the role of the laity in the Church (including their formation in the faith) he foreshadowed the Second Vatican Council, which has been called 'Newman's Council'. Some of that emphasis was expressed in sermons of his in the beautiful church he built in Dublin when he was rector of the Catholic University.

Nearly all of his vast literary output is prose. His style has been called 'cloistral'. Two of the many examples of this are the description of the Mass in his novel *Loss and Gain* and the prayer for a happy death, often seen on memorial cards. The style could also be called 'thoughtful or full of thought'; it is not always easy reading. His *Apologia Pro Vita Sua*, an autobiographical account of the history of his mind, was a meticulous and massive response to an attack on his own integrity in particular and on that of the Catholic clergy in general. Written under pressure and published in instalments, it was a bestseller and a boost for the Catholic Church in the English-speaking world, especially in England.

His two most famous poems are 'Lead, Kindly Light', written in the aftermath of a mentally disturbing illness and in the lead-up to the Oxford Movement; and 'The Dream of Gerontius' from his Catholic period, an epic poem about the soul crossing the frontier of death, afterwards set to superb music by Elgar.

César Auguste Franck (1822–1890) was Belgian-born but spent nearly all his life in Paris. We might say that his main musical home was the organ loft of the church of Sainte Clothilde where he was organist and choir master. His lyrical romanticist music echoes the rhapsodic improvisations beloved of organists. He was a man of strong faith; music to him was a kind of prayer. His major work on a religious theme is the oratorio *The Beatitudes*, an appropriate subject for one who believed as he did.

There are two special memorials of him: the École César Franck in Paris, which promotes quality Catholic church music, and his setting for *Panis Angelicus*, very probably composed in the presence of the Blessed Sacrament, frequently performed, still deepening faith and lifting the heart.

Words and music fill our world of sense
words on our lips, music from instruments
they mean far more than surface hearing, seeing
they're stirrings of the soul, of deep down being.

It is revealed that God is truly Word
can God be praised as Melody, as Chord?
Father, Son and Spirit, Blessed Three
are They the ultimate in harmony?

Poet, Composer, help us read your score
be our words and music forevermore.

THE NUN OF NORMANDY

THÉRÈSE

In the 1840s, a young man named Louis Martin presented himself at a monastery in Switzerland and asked to be admitted as a postulant. He was told to apply himself to Latin first. He applied himself to Greek as well, then changed his mind and resumed his training in watch-making, going on to set up as a watch-maker and jeweller in his native Alençon in Normandy.

Zélie Guérin asked to be accepted as a postulant with the Daughters of Charity. She was told that she had no vocation to them and she set up as a lace-maker in Alençon. She noticed Louis one day in 1858 on one of the town bridges and discreetly ensured that he noticed her. A few months later they were married.

They had nine children, of whom five daughters survived into adulthood. Their last child was born on 2 January 1873 and was christened Marie Francoise Thérèse. She almost died in infancy and owed her life to Rose Taille, a farmer's wife who cared for her for over a year.

The baby of the family received from and contributed to the religious and affectionate atmosphere of the comfortable middle-class home. Louis had been able to retire from watch-making and assisted in his wife's lace-making business. Not surprisingly, they idolised the 'new arrival', but Zélie's worship of her daughter was cut short by her death from cancer in 1877. The widower and his five daughters moved to Lisieux and settled down in a substantial suburban property where they lived a reserved life: materially comfortable, unworldly in spirit, strongly Catholic and deeply united.

On the religious side, apart from basics like sacraments and prayer, Thérèse's upbringing included her 'Pranzini experience': the unrepentant murderer for whom she and her sister Céline prayed and made sacrifices, and who suddenly kissed the crucifix on the scaffold and exchanged a few words with the chaplain; and her belief that Our Lady appeared to her 'beautiful, so beautiful' and healed her of a distressing illness.

Between her and her father there was a rapport beyond the ordinary. Her sister Pauline, to whom she was very close, joined the Lisieux Carmel, to be followed a few years later by her sister Marie. The fourteen-year-old Thérèse told her father that she wished to enter Carmel very soon. He agreed.

However, the diocesan superior of the Carmel did not. He asked her to wait until she was twenty-one, adding that she could appeal to the bishop. So she went with her father, with her hair put up to make her look older, to state her case to the bishop for joining Carmel at the age of fifteen. Shortly afterwards, Pope Leo XIII experienced something new in papal audiences when a young pilgrim, against all protocol, in words supplied by her Carmelite sister, asked him to let her enter Carmel at the age of fifteen. He diplomatically said that she would if it was God's will. The bishop decided that it was his will too, and so three months after her fifteenth birthday the Carmel door opened to her.

Her vow day, delayed by a still cautious diocesan superior, was 8 September 1890. She soon showed charity and competence in an influenza epidemic that swept the community. In 1893 she had her last meeting with her father, by then paralysed and mentally impaired and soon to die. After his death Céline made the fourth Martin in the convent.

Life in Carmel was very austere, especially to one used to material comfort. What she found hardest to bear physically was the cold: 'I have suffered from cold' she said on her death-bed 'until I thought I would die of it.' She was a great believer in and practiser of unspectacular self-denial out of love for Christ. It was part of the life-pattern she had committed herself to: 'I have come to save souls and to pray for priests', she said before her vows when asked officially why she had come to Carmel.

She spoke of that life-pattern as her 'little way ... the path of confidence and complete surrender.' In her own case, her following of 'the little way' must have been illumined by the assurance of her confessor that she had never committed a mortal sin. Novice-mistress in fact if not in name, she schooled the novices in 'the little way', insisting that it was a way of sacrifice.

She wrote many poems that are rich in her spirituality. She often composed them during the day in her head and wrote them down in her evening free time. She was quite a letter writer: to her relatives and to the seminarian and priest (her 'missionary brothers' as she called them), whose spiritual sister she became in obedience to Pauline, then prioress.

Also in obedience to Pauline she wrote a memoir, mostly of her life before she entered Carmel. Pauline's order was more important than she realised; the work done in Thérèse's spare time on the inferior copybook paper was to become the first part of *The Story of a Soul*, the book that established her fame, spread her message and led to her canonisation. The climax of this 'Part One' of her story is the offering of herself as a victim to the merciful love of God.

'Part Two' begins as a letter to her sister Marie, but develops into a prayer of love to the Lord. Its most famous section is where she sees herself as belonging to the heart of the Body of Christ, the Church. 'Part Three' was ordered by and addressed to Marie de Gonzague, successor to Pauline as prioress. It deals with her life in Carmel, ranging from simple human happenings to spiritual darkness. She stopped writing early in July 1897 because she could write no more – she was dying of pulmonary tuberculosis. The final word in all three manuscripts is 'love'.

Thus followed three months of great physical pain and great aridity of spirit. The 'little way' in this period must surely have been the way of the cross. She died on the evening of 30 September. The 'Era of Thérèse' in the life of the Church was soon to begin.

Like Bede, a person of one place
like Xavier, saint of global grace
a surging of desire
to set the world on fire

Apostle of the little way
of quiet surrender day by day
not always in the light
she knew tormented night
Hold on, hold on, love more and more
a mesh of grace and will: adore
a touch of Joan of Arc
'Jesu' from the dark

September evening, setting sun
day is over, day's begun
her words still leap and flame
millions bless her name.

PART II

Twentieth-Century Testimony

LABOURER IN LOVE

MATT TALBOT

'An elderly man collapsed in Granby Lane yesterday and on being taken to Jervis Street Hospital was found to be dead. He was wearing a tweed suit but there was nothing to identify who he was' (*Irish Independent*, Monday, 8 June 1925). Susan Fylan identified the remains as those of her brother Matthew ('Matt') Talbot.

He was born into the family of Charles Talbot and Elizabeth Bagnall on 22 May 1856. The Talbots lived in the north of Dublin ('northsiders'), part of Dublin's teeming population of poor, many of them in tenements.

Matt was a pupil at two schools run by the Irish Christian Brothers, spending a year at each, mostly learning his four 'Rs' – reading, 'riting, 'rithmetic and religion – and making his first confession, first communion and confirmation. The roll or attendance record of one of the schools notes him as a 'mitcher'. The 'mitcher' became a messenger with a wine and bottling firm and then with the Dublin Port and Docks Board. After that he became a bricklayer's labourer, acquiring a reputation as a first-rate hodman. He moved from one job to another until he acquired permanent employment with T. and C. Martin, timber merchants.

Very soon he became addicted to alcohol. Nearly all his wages were spent on drink. He pawned, odd-jobbed and collected bottles to get money for it. 'He only wanted one thing – the drink', a companion said. He himself went on to confess: 'When I was young I was very careless about religion because of drink and I broke my mother's heart'.

Excessive drinking was a major part of his environment and of his home. Nearly all the Talbot men were heavy drinkers and public houses were very numerous in their neighbourhoods. It was an accepted system in Dublin that many workers were paid in pubs either in cash or by cheque or order cashed by the management. Predictably, pubs prospered and families suffered.

It was noted that 'though he did curse and profane the Holy Name, he did not use impure language', and that though he neglected communion he never missed Sunday Mass and held Our Lady in honour. 'I heard him say,' testified his sister, 'that even when he was drinking he was devout in his mind to the Blessed Virgin and used to say an odd Hail Mary and he attributed his conversion to this.'

Matt's moment of truth came one Saturday pay day when, moneyless after some workless days, he realised that none of his friends were going to treat him to a drink. He went home and announced that he was going to take the pledge. It was a momentous weekend: Saturday: 'no treat', confession, pledge; Sunday: Mass and Communion; Monday: Mass at dawn – it was the dawn of a new life.

His life became one of penance – the first penance being to keep the pledge. 'I'll never stick it', he told his mother. But he did, surely largely through the prayers of this long-suffering and remarkable woman. He renewed his pledge for another period and then for life, and finally, on 4 May 1890 as member number 113, he made his 'Heroic Offering' in the Total Abstinence League of the Sacred Heart, which in 1899 became the Pioneer Association.

His family and companions heard no more bad or profane language from him; he wore two crossed pins on his cuff to help him in that regard. There was no more smoking – a big thing to give up. He slept on a plank bed and wooden pillow and wore chains next to his skin. (It was the finding of these chains on his dead body that led to public notice of him.) In his austerity he very much reflected the Irish tradition of holiness as union with Christ in his Passion.

It was a eucharistic life: Mass every morning and (when he was in T. and C. Martin's) another Mass on his way to work, a feast of Masses on Sunday and daily visits to the Blessed Sacrament. Presumably he became a daily communicant, at least after Pope Saint Pius X's decree on frequent communion in 1905.

It was a life of prayer: apart from his time spent in church, there was prolonged prayer at home, morning and evening, and prayer at free moments in his workplace. He told a friend that he had received the gift of prayer.

The church he frequented most was the Jesuit church in Gardiner Street, where his accustomed place to pray was near the then Saint Joseph's altar; but in a sense his 'moment of truth' home was Clonliffe College, where he had taken his original pledge and which he visited regularly for confession and spiritual direction.

One of the most remarkable facts about his new life was his reading list. This man had spent only two years at primary school (and that interspersed with mitching), so his reading must have been minimal. Now he amassed a considerable library almost entirely of religious works, some his own, others loaned to him: the Bible, lives of the saints, Church history, treatises, tracts on social issues and so on. Authors included Saint Augustine, Saint Thomas Aquinas, Saint Teresa of Avila, Newman, Faber and Belloc. The mitcher had come a long way.

He was especially attracted to the Passion, to the gospel named after his namesake, who also left worldly things and followed Jesus, and to the life of Augustine; no doubt he saw parallels between the sinner-saint and himself and between Monica and his own mother, whose heart he felt he had broken. He told a workmate that he often asked the Holy Spirit to give him his understanding of what he read.

His reading on social matters reflects the industrial ferment in Dublin in the early 1900s. Unskilled labour was over-plentiful and therefore cheap. In 1908 the Irish Transport and General Workers' Union was founded for casual and unskilled workers with the dynamic James ('Big Jim') Larkin as its financial secretary. Strikes and lockouts led to the great confrontation of 1913. The Employers' Federation, led by the tramways and newspaper magnate William Murphy, refused to employ ITGWU members and drafted an agreement (aimed at sympathetic strikes) whereby workers undertook to handle goods from any source. T. and C. Martin became involved. The men refused to sign the agreement and came out on strike, Matt among them.

He did not picket; apparently older men were not asked to. Remarks he made indicate that he admired and trusted Larkin and that he believed workers should have a better wage. (One of the best things Larkin did was to have the cashing of pay cheques in pubs abolished.)

So the years passed for the small, wiry man with the sloping shoulders and the long stride. There are testimonies to his honesty and truthfulness (two of his great virtues), his direct manner, the odd flare of temper, the help for his friends in need and for Church charities, as well as the work well done.

But 'Brother Ass' was giving up. In 1923 he had two stints in hospital. For over a year he was unemployed and extremely poor. In 1925 he returned to Martin's. He 'clocked out' on Saturday, 6 June. The following day (Trinity Sunday) he attended his sodality Mass and Communion in the Jesuit church. Later that morning he set out for another Mass and collapsed a few yards from the Dominican church. Time to 'clock in'.

> *Drain the glass: fill it up*
> *to the brim*
> *Other thirst: take His cup*
> *drink with Him*
> *Carry wood: serve the boss*
> *every day*
> *Other wood: share His Cross*
> *all the way*
> *Listening heart: hear His call*
> *day and night*
> *Run to Mass: stumble, fall*
> *into light.*

TORINESE

PIER-GIORGIO FRASSATI

On 7 June 1925, a group of students climbed La Lunelle in the Italian Alps. On the summit they prayed for a student who had died on the mountain the previous year. The young man who suggested the prayers had only a month to live.

Pier-Giorgio Frassati was born on 6 April 1901 into a wealthy Turin family. His father was owner-manager of the liberal daily newspaper *La Stampa*, becoming in 1913 a senator of Italy and after the First World War Italian ambassador in Berlin.

After tuition at home, Pier-Giorgio went to the Massimo D'Azeglio school and the Jesuit social institute, and then to the Royal Polytechnic of Turin for the degree of mining engineer. He was a great 'joiner': the Sodality of Our Lady; the Balbo Circle of the Federation of Catholic University Students; the Society of Saint Vincent de Paul; the Dominican Third Order; a Blessed Sacrament adoration group; the Italian People's Party (the forerunner of the Christian Democrats).

His membership of these organisations was no mere formality but an expression of a deep faith-commitment. His membership of the adoration group, the Sodality and the Saint Vincent de Paul Society especially point to three great loves of his life: the Eucharistic Christ, Our Lady and the poor.

At eleven years of age he began to receive the Eucharist several times a week. At seventeen he became a daily communicant. People began to notice this young man lost in prayer before and after communion. (After his death a plaque in his memory was set up in his parish church near where he used to kneel.) It was noticed too that when leaving a church he would make a gesture of farewell towards the tabernacle. People in Pollone where his family had a country house became aware of the horse (an Irish horse) stopping instinctively outside the church and the rider making a sign of the Cross and bowing low. On mountaineering expeditions at weekends he tried to ensure that the group would have Mass on the way.

As regards Our Lady, he united his daily communion with a daily rosary. He celebrated his entry into her sodality with weekly fresh roses for her shrine during the month of May. He was a frequent pilgrim climber to her shrine at Oropa. As with the Eucharist, his devotion to her was not only a private affair; he proclaimed her at the top of his voice saying the rosary in public processions – no small thing at a time of widespread anti-Catholicism.

His love for the poor went back to his childhood and flowered in the Society of Saint Vincent de Paul. There is story after story of his extraordinary empathy with them. 'He created his own family among the poor and unfortunate', a friend said, seeing in him something of Saint Francis of Assisi.

He himself saw his service of the poor as a thanksgiving for Holy Communion. Perhaps the most moving memento of him is the note he scrawled in agony the day before he died to his co-visitor for two poor clients: 'Here are the injections for Converso. The [pawnshop] receipt is Sappa's ... redeem it.'

This handsome and attractive young man was a born leader. He had a great gaiety and a capacity for relaxing with people. For him real friendship involved Christ. 'He always put Our Lord between himself and us like a sort of hyphen', a friend wrote. Aelred of Rievaulx would have approved. There are testimonies to the engracing effect of even his presence.

He received no encouragement in his religious life from his parents. His father was an unbeliever and his mother was a Catholic of minimal observance. Both of these highly capable people were disappointed in their son and heir, who seemed to be frittering away his time and whose scholastic results were bad (study was not his forte). His father berated him for not taking life 'seriously' but sensed in him a strange maturity. The young man did bear the imprint of his father's tenacity and honesty and of the spartan training given to him by his mother, but it was enriched in a way beyond their understanding.

Father and son were united in their detestation of fascism. When Mussolini came to power in 1922 the father resigned his ambassadorship. Later he gave up directing his newspaper (its liberalism was of course anathema to the new government) and sold it for a song. The son strongly protested the decision of the president of the Balbo Circle to honour a visit of Mussolini to Turin. When fascist thugs invaded the Frassati home, he tackled the would-be telephone wire cutter and the gang fled.

In the summer of 1925 he was preparing for his final diploma. Crisis came in mounting waves of pain: headache, fatigue, increasing immobility. The definitive diagnosis was terminal poliomyelitis. He had told his friends: 'I think that the most beautiful day of my life will be the day of my death'. This 'most beautiful day' was 4 July 1925.

> *Friends on the hills: laughter and song*
> *day to remember long*
>
> *Friends in Turin: hear, understand*
> *day of the helping hand*
>
> *Friend in the church; offer, be fed*
> *day of the living Bread*
>
> *Friend in the heart; barriers fall*
> *day that is best of all.*

IN THE NAME OF THE KING

MIGUEL PRO JUÁREZ

Miguel Pro Juárez was born on 13 January 1891. His father was a wealthy Mexican mine owner. When he was about twenty, his mother, Josepha Juárez, persuaded him to make a retreat to get over his upset at his sisters' decisions to become nuns. He returned from the retreat and announced that he was going to join the Jesuits. He took his vows in 1913.

Then the history of Mexico caught up with him in the shape of a civil war between the adherents of the president Huerta and those of the United States-supported Carranza. The Carrancistas captured Mexico's second largest city, Guadalajara, where Miguel's mother and her family (the father's whereabouts were unknown) had taken refuge and the novitiate community, including Miguel, had re-gathered. Jesuit authority judged that Mexico was unsafe for him and his companions and sent them to Los Gatos in California to begin their studies.

Further studies brought Miguel twice to Spain (with a teaching period in Nicaragua between philosophy and theology) and then to Enghien in Belgium for social studies – he was interested in apostolate among workers. He was ordained priest there in 1925. Ill health with three operations had not destroyed his innate gaiety.

His writing reveals a deep sense of priesthood: 'This something that I find within me and I had never felt before ... is the divine mark that the Holy Spirit imprints on the soul when he gives us the priestly character ... Whatever good I happened to accomplish was all due to the grace of the priesthood, to the Holy Spirit ... to that something ... which I had not felt before the day I was ordained.'

His mother died in early 1926. Later that year he arrived back in Mexico. Once more Mexican history and his life interlocked. Battle lines between Church and State, or rather between the Catholic people and the government, were drawn.

The Carrancistas had enacted a constitution with a strong anti-religious slant. The Church was to be outlawed from primary schools, religious real property was to become State property with places of worship publicly supervised; the various Mexican states could limit their number of ministers of religion.

Carranza fought shy of fully implementing these previsions. He died by assassination. He was succeeded by Obregon, the victor of Guadalajara, who started to harass the Church and in 1924 passed the presidential baton to Plutarcho Calles, who had none of Carranza's shyness. The Mexican Nero had arrived.

His attempt to create a State-controlled bishopless Church came to nothing. But various Church-run institutions were closed, a sort of ministry to administer seized Church property was set up, the number of ministering priests was much reduced, all foreign priests and many bishops were expelled.

There was a strong Catholic resistance. The National League for the Defence of Religious Liberty was active with propaganda, legal protest and boycott. In some areas Catholics resorted to armed action. These were the Cristeros with their battle cry, 'Long live Christ the King', derived from the feast of the Kingship, instituted by Pope Pius XI in 1925. A leading light of League and Cristeros was the charismatic Anacleto Flores Gonzalez, who was executed a few months before Miguel's arrival. His last public words became one of the great texts in the history of the Church in Latin America: 'Let the Americas hear it again: I die but God lives. Long live Christ the King'.

The bishops came to the dramatic decision, approved by the Pope, to withdraw from the churches rather than submit them to State control: 'All rites, all public religious functions requiring the participation of a priest shall be suspended in all the churches of the republic'. The imminence of interdict meant a virtually non-stop ministry for priests to cope with the thousands coming to receive the sacraments. Miguel played his part. On 31 July 1926, the sanctuary lamps all over Mexico were quenched.

From then on his life reads like a thriller, a hark back to the catacombs, to Tudor England: Mass in private houses, passwords, whispered rituals. He organised 'Eucharistic Stations' at which he distributed Holy Communion, visited prisoners, cared for the poor and gave camouflaged retreats, including one to taxi drivers with the retreat-giver disguised as a mechanic.

He conducted this remarkable ministry with a certain aplomb and derring-do, conveyed in a famous photograph of him almost literally under the presidential nose: in lounge suit and straw hat, moustached, in casual pose with cigarette in hand, and behind him a Calles guard and Calles' official residence.

And so to November 1927. Bombs were thrown at Obregon's car. He was virtually unhurt. The police alleged that one of the assailants, wounded and in hospital and thinking he was among friends, said: 'Tell Father Pro Juárez and his brother Humberto and Luis Segura Vilchis to hide'. Miguel and his brothers Humberto and Roberto were arrested and brought to the prefecture of police. Also imprisoned were Vilchis (one of the young men Miguel had been training for Catholic leadership) and the teenager Tirado, a mere witness of the bombing. There was no judicial process.

On 23 November all of them, except Roberto, were brought into the garden of the prefecture to an area used for shooting practice. Photographs still extant show Miguel kneeling in prayer and standing with arms extended facing the firing squad. They do not of course record what he reportedly said just before they fired, words spoken with the quiet but distinct intonation that he used for the consecration in the Mass: 'Hail, Christ the King'.

The funeral was a massive protest and celebration. The Calles government did not dare to intervene. 'There is nothing here to weep for', said the father of the two brothers. The Father-General of the Jesuits announced to them 'the joyful news of Father Miguel Pro's glorious death for Christ'.

Miguel peregrino:
miner's son, Josepha's boy
from coast to coast a race to run
into priestly joy

Miguel caballero:
serve the King in Calles' night
till Christ comes royally welcoming
into blessed light.

THE PRIEST WHO WAS HARD ON HIMSELF

JOHN SULLIVAN

The nurse broke the news to her patient that her cancer was incurable. The woman said that she would go to Father John Sullivan of Clongowes Wood College, County Kildare, with the hope of a cure. The nurse asked what was special about him. 'He is very hard on himself,' the patient said, 'You would have to be hard on yourself to work miracles. And he does it.'

John Sullivan grew up in the privileged, mainly Protestant upper-class society of nineteenth-century Dublin. His father, Edward, was a well-known lawyer climbing the social and legal ladder on his way to a baronetcy and the Lord Chancellorship of Ireland. His mother was Elizabeth Bailey of a wealthy Cork family. In keeping with the practice of the time in inter-faith marriages, her four sons were reared Protestants and one daughter was brought up a Catholic.

John, the youngest of the family, was born on 8 May 1861 at 41 Eccles Street in north Dublin. He was baptised in the nearby Saint George's Church on 15 July and while he was still a baby the family moved to 32 Fitzwilliam Place, on the opposite side of the city. They lived for part of the year in Killiney, County Dublin, which became a place of tragedy for them in 1877 when the second son, Robert, was drowned in a boating accident.

After six years in Portora Royal School in County Fermanagh, John went to Trinity College, Dublin, got his BA and enrolled in Trinity law school. After his father's death in 1885 he went to London, studied at Lincoln's Inn and was called to the English Bar.

Not much is known of his legal work. He seems to have had no great desire for a legal career. He hardly needed to; his father had left him with ample means. Good-natured and of serious mind, with an 'apartness' that was to be a life characteristic, the tall, impeccably dressed John Sullivan with the very blue eyes and thick hair moved quietly in his own circle of Dublin polite society (with, it seems, his sister keeping an eye on mothers aspiring to be mothers-in-law), apparently destined to live out his life in that privileged world.

The apartness was expressed in the long tours in Switzerland, Turkey and Greece which provided him with memories that he shared on occasion: his stay with the monks of Mount Athos, the bandit he bought off with a packet of cigarettes and Morfeios the Mayor who turned out to be a descendant of Murphy the exile. The apartness may also have indicated that he was being drawn towards a more meaningful life; he did correspond with Mount Athos and there was an impression that he was thinking of becoming a monk there.

There are one or two 'straws in the wind' regarding his move towards Catholicism. He recalled long afterwards the Catholic servant in Trinity who used to urge the students to go to church on Sundays. John told her that church-going meant nothing to him, but that he would go to her church with her. They went to Mass together but we do not know what his impressions were or whether he went again. We do know that he took a great interest in the catechism lessons of a little girl in Glencar in Kerry where he was on holiday and that he attended Mass during his time there.

But there is no doubt that he was convinced that he owed his Catholic faith to the prayers and example of his mother. In 1913 he wrote to a bereaved mother: 'I owe everything in the world to my mother's prayers and so know the power of a mother's prayers, especially in the hour of sorrow ... to her prayers at that time [of the Killiney tragedy] and to her resignation to God's will I believe I owe everything.' His devotion to Saint Augustine and Saint Monica points to the same conviction, and in a piece he wrote shortly before his death he applied Augustine's acknowledgement of his spiritual debt to his mother to himself. When she died in 1898 he poured lilies into her grave.

By that time he was a Catholic. He was received into the Church on 21 December 1896 at the Jesuit Farm Street church in London and into the Sodality of Our Lady the following day. He took 'Francis' as his confirmation name: whether it was 'of Assisi' or 'Xavier' we do not know for certain.

On his return to Dublin he rid his room of its fine fittings and himself of his fine clothes: the couple of dozen stylish ties (he had been fussy about ties) shrank to a few plain ones and his silk underwear disappeared. He became a visitor to convents, to a hospice for the dying and to schools for the poor, making new friends. He was at Mass every day. The 'new' John Sullivan had arrived, providing some drawing-rooms with a new subject of conversation.

There is evidence that he intended to join the Capuchins (does this indicate that the saint of Assisi was the confirmation 'Francis' and the inspiration of his new simplicity of life?), but certain nuns (and perhaps others) steered him towards the Society of Jesus. He entered the Jesuit novitiate in 1900. At his vows two years later he took as his 'vow crucifix' a crucifix that had belonged to his mother. He was to use it much in his ministry. It is now the best-known relic of him and is constantly brought to help the sick.

He was ordained priest in 1907 and was assigned to Clongowes Wood College. Apart from tertianship (spiritual year) and five years as rector of the community at Rathfarnham, Dublin, he spent the rest of his life there. Already he was known as a man of deep prayer and of great, if at times embarrassing, humility and charity. But it was the Clongowes years that brought this very private person to public notice. The word spread that besides being a 'holy man' he had the gift of healing. Many in distress came to him. And he went to them; the priest in the much-mended clothes half-running along or on an ancient bicycle became a familiar figure in the surrounding countryside. Dublin hospitals and nursing homes knew him too.

He ministered simply and straightforwardly, no dramatics, no 'hype'. Much prayer, use of a relic, the sprinkling of holy or Lourdes water, the enjoining of prayer and an act of self-denial was the general pattern. Many bodily healings were attributed to him; spiritual healings too. There were occasions when, though there was no cure, pain and distress ceased.

He brought gifts to the poor and ran small accounts for them in one or two local shops. He befriended the travelling people and there is a Caravaggian/Rembrandtesque scene of him officiating by lantern light at the funeral of a homeless man with residents of the Celbridge county home as gravediggers.

He was not the best of teachers, overestimating the boys' learning abilities, labelling even small misdemeanours 'audacious' (a favourite word of his). But with the intuition of the young they sensed his goodness, sincerity and concern for them, both as teacher and 'spiritual father'. They may not have grasped all he said in classroom, chapel or confessional, but what he was did make an impact. The many religious he gave retreats to had the same impression of him.

Like that of his contemporary and fellow Dubliner Matt Talbot, his life was very austere: the sparsely-furnished room with an apology of a fire in winter, the mended clothes, the shortened sleep, the minimal diet (which he obediently augmented in later years). Like Matt he had a special devotion to the Heart and Passion of Christ and to the Blessed Sacrament and to Our Lady. On walks he would hold his hat in one hand and say his Rosary on the beads into it. When approaching a church he would put on his hat so as to salute the Blessed Sacrament. He was a prayer-filled man.

Though his conversation often ran on sad subjects, he had a sense of humour, a fund of witty anecdotes and a 'cheer up, cheer up, cheer up' for the despondent. He took an interest in others. His kindness was proverbial. But there was always the apartness. It has been said that the only bad thing about him was his handwriting; at first almost copper-plate, it deteriorated into virtual indecipherability.

He died holding his vow crucifix on 19 February 1933 in a nursing home a street's length away from Fitzwilliam Place. For years his remains lay at Clongowes among the people he served. Now they rest in the Jesuit Church in Dublin, a few streets away from where he was born and baptised.

THE PRIEST WHO WAS HARD ON HIMSELF

Man of duality:
cyclist in style along Stillorgan Road
pedaller in patches in a country lane
climber in Greece, half-runner in Kildare
man-about-town becoming wide awake
making the break
living in prayer
healing the pain
sharing the load
loving audaciously.

A LITTLE SLIP OF A MAN

TITUS BRANDSMA

Anno-Sjoerd Brandsma was born of farming folk at Oegeklooster, Friesland, in the northern Netherlands on 23 February 1881. He was of delicate health and small build; his father called him 'a little slip of a man'. He had an intellectual, indeed a contemplative, disposition and it was no great surprise when he joined the Carmelites. They gave him the name Titus. After ordination he was sent to Rome for a doctorate, then back to the Netherlands to a life of seminary academia, local journalism and overseeing and management of Catholic schools.

In 1923 the Catholic University of the Netherlands was established by royal decree. Titus was appointed its professor in the departments of theology, philosophy and history (including the history of mysticism). In 1932/1933 the 'little slip of a man' had a more resounding title: 'Rector Magnificus' of the University. (During his term of office the man who was to overshadow his last years also gained an impressive title – Adolf Hitler became Chancellor of Germany.)

For this busy sickness-prone, high-profile figure in Dutch education and journalism, the 'inner things' were a priority. 'My Mass in the early morning is my half hour of happiness', he said. Saint Teresa's 'Interior Castle' was his 'breviary'. And the inner things shone outwardly: 'He passed by,' someone said, 'like a ray of sunshine.'

In September 1939 the Second World War began, but the Netherlands remained neutral. In May 1940 Germany launched a *blitzkrieg* on the Netherlands and occupied the country. With the cooperation of the National Socialist Movement (the Dutch counterpart of the Nazi party), the new administrators began to apply their anti-religious and racist policies, with education as one of their targets. The salaries of teachers of religion were drastically reduced. Religious were not to be in charge of schools and Jewish pupils were to be expelled. Titus strongly opposed all of this.

The regime also ruled that only National Socialist Movement advertisements and articles (and pieces approved by them) were to appear in newspapers, including Church-run publications. Titus, as press adviser to the Cardinal Archbishop of Utrecht, urged him, and through him the Dutch hierarchy, to stand firm. They did. They issued a pastoral letter to say that Catholic papers would not carry Nazi articles or propaganda. It was officially a statement of the bishops, but the Nazi authorities knew who had inspired it. Titus was promptly arrested.

While in custody he wrote what amounted to a testament of his gospel-based commitment to truth and freedom and worked on a biography of Saint Teresa of Avila. The 'inner things', including his rosary said on a cross-marked button, remained of course a priority, but we gather that, like Thérèse in her last days, he experienced spiritual darkness.

At first he was sentenced to imprisonment in the Netherlands until the end of the war. Then the venue was changed: he was to go to the dreaded Dachau near Munich. There he became number 30492 in a regime that was brutal and deliberately dehumanising. Some elements were grotesque, surreal: the 'Work Makes You Free' motto over the gate, crematoria flanked by flowers and background music for executions.

The prisoners in Titus' unit, blending courage and caution, maintained religious practice, managing even to administer and receive Holy Communion. On one occasion, when a guard knocked him to the ground, his main concern was to keep a tight grip on his spectacles case, not to save his glasses, but because it contained the Blessed Sacrament. (The two most famous occasions of sacramental worship in Dachau were on 17 December 1944, when deacon Karl Leisner, a former youth leader and mortally ill of imprisonment and tuberculosis, was secretly ordained by a French prisoner-bishop, Gabriel Piguet, and on 26 December 1944, when he secretly celebrated Mass. He was released in May 1945 and died three months later.)

In the camp hospital Titus was subjected to medical experimentation. He managed to receive the sacrament of the sick. Through the good offices of the imprisoned Fritz Kuhr, once secretary to Heinrich Brüning, Catholic Chancellor of Germany 1930–1932, he received viaticum. He was killed by injection on 26 July 1942, two weeks before Edith Stein died in Auschwitz. The broken body of 'the little slip of a man' was cremated and what was left was routinely disposed of.

Friesland farm and Friesland sea
ethos of work and liberty
lots of faith, hope, charity
for a little slip of a man

Carmel: called to holiness
priest: to sacrifice, to bless
fighter: freedom of the press
this little slip of a man

Dachau: horror through and through
prisoner three-o-four-nine-two
a number now, no longer you
a little slip of a man

Even here the shafts of grace
Jesus comes in a spectacles case
forevermore a love embrace
for a little slip of a man

WOMAN FOR TRUTH

EDITH TERESA STEIN

One day in 1921, a thirty-year-old German Jewish woman of brilliant intellect opened a book, read it far into the night and closed it, saying, 'This is the truth'. The book was the autobiography of the great Carmelite Saint Teresa of Avila; the woman was Edith Stein.

She was born on 12 October 1891 in the then German city of Breslau (now Wroclaw in Poland) into a large and wealthy Jewish family in the timber business. The family was strongly religious but she became an atheist in her teens, giving up prayer. Bookish from childhood, in her late teens she enrolled in the University of Breslau where she enjoyed the academic and social life. Then she moved to the University of Gottingen for philosophy. There she was in her element in the circle around Edmund Husserl, the distinguished philosopher of the time and the father of phenomenology. She became his favourite student and graduate and also his assistant.

Philosophy for her was a serious pursuit of truth and she began to realise that the full truth lay beyond what philosophy could give. 'I had not yet begun to pray,' she wrote later, 'but this longing for truth was in itself a prayer.' And Christian influences began to make themselves felt.

At the Gottingen she noticed that many devotees of philosophy were also devoted Christians. An ancient version of the 'Our Father' which she discovered in her studies made an impact. There was the serene faith of her ex-tutor's widow after the death of her husband in the First World War; they had converted from Judaism to Protestant Christianity. This faith of her friend, we gather, gave Edith something like Paul's Damascus road experience. And finally Saint Teresa had her say.

She was baptised on 1 January 1922, taking the name Teresa. She knelt before her mother and said, 'I am a Catholic'. This woman, a widow of many years, who combined strong religious observance and business acumen and who had done so much for the baby of the family, never fully accepted the conversion. This must have been an element of pain in the joy of the new Christian.

Edith became a teacher in a Dominican teacher training college. She came into demand as a speaker at Catholic gatherings, coming across as thoughtful, articulate, prayerful, unworldly and charitable. She had a special devotion to the Blessed Sacrament and (probably with a presentiment of peril) to Our Lady of Sorrows.

Presentiment turned to reality early in 1933 when the fanatically anti-Semitic Nazis swept into power under Adolf Hitler. Her frightened employers at the Institute of Educational Theory in Münster had to let her go. She felt deeply for 'my people'. She wrote to Pope Pius XI asking him to speak out on behalf of the Jews, warning that what was happening to them would happen to Catholics too. Perhaps her letter helped the Pope to issue his hard-hitting anti-Nazi encyclical in 1937.

Later in 1933 she joined the Carmelites of Cologne – it was the fulfilment of a baptismal dream. It was only too clear that Sister Teresa Benedicta was not much good at sewing and house work. It was also clear, if only from the small library she arrived with, that an intellectual was in their midst. Happily, the prioress encouraged her to write, which she did: she completed her *Finite and Eternal Being*, an attempt to synthesise the philosophy of Saint Thomas Aquinas and modern thought, especially phenomenology. It can be seen as her act of homage to the two great thinkers who had helped to mould her mind: the Dominican doctor of the Church and the beloved guru of Gottingen. But she could not find a firm brave or rash enough to publish a book written by a Jew.

The Nazi government passed one anti-Semitic law after another: Jews lost citizenship and voting rights, were forbidden to marry Germans (Aryans), were barred from various occupations and required to wear yellow badges. Third Reich reality was literally brought home to the Cologne Carmelites when officials arrived with ballot boxes to enable the sisters to vote, since, the officials said (incorrectly), they were not allowed to go out to vote. Sister Stein was duly noted as a 'non-Aryan' and denied the franchise.

Then came 9 November 1938. In a devastating reprisal for the murder by a Jew of an official of the German embassy in Paris, synagogues went up in flames, Jewish shops and homes were attacked and looted and many Jews were arrested. It was called *'kristallnacht'* because of all the smashed windows. Some weeks later Edith Teresa and her sister Rosa, who had become a Catholic, crossed the frontier into the Netherlands.

At the end of 1938, Edith escaped into the Netherlands to her new home, the Carmel at Echt. Her sister Rosa, by now a Catholic and about to become a Third Order Carmelite, joined her there in 1940. About the same time the Germans invaded and occupied the hitherto neutral Netherlands. The spectre of Nazi anti-Semitism began to stalk the land of canals and windmills. The Stein sisters were no longer safe. Could Edith Teresa join a Carmel in neutral Switzerland? At last she got the 'green light' to go, but she would not go without Rosa who had become a Carmelite tertiary. A Swiss haven was found for her too and Swiss civil authorities were approached.

Against this background of tension and threat she lived her life of prayer and wrote her best known work, *The Science of the Cross*, which was a presentation of the life and teaching of Saint John of the Cross. She worked on it for the best part of a year, probably with the thought that it might well be her last book. The SS arrived at the convent on 2 August 1942. A last prayer before the Blessed Sacrament, a hurried farewell to the community with an urgent word to try to get last-minute Swiss consular protection for Rosa and herself, the short walk to the car: an episode of about ten minutes. They were two of the victims of Nazi retaliation for the determined public protest of the Dutch Catholic bishops against the persecution of the Jews. By this time Nazi racism had gone far beyond shattered windows and yellow badges; the unspeakable 'Final Solution' was in operation.

She was seen helping her co-prisoners at a camp in the northern Netherlands. She was seen and spoken to on an east-bound train at a railway halt in Germany. A few written words survive from that terrible journey: 'On the way to Poland, with love from Sister Teresa Benedicta. Praying marvellously so far'. The prayerless adolescent atheist had come a long way. She died with many others at Auschwitz on 9 August 1942.

SO GREAT A CLOUD

Another Ruth
to glean the field of truth
spouse of Christ
like him sacrificed
east to the sun
to join the Risen One.

THE MAN WHO SAID NO

FRANZ JÄGERSTÄTTER

Braunau in Upper Austria is part of history as the birthplace of Adolf Hitler. Twenty miles away is the village of Saint Radegund, the birthplace and burial place of the peasant farmer who said no to the dictator whose armies had conquered so much of Europe.

Franz Jägerstätter was born outside of marriage on 20 May 1907. His father was killed in the First World War. His mother married and when the marriage proved childless her husband adopted Franz. When Franz married he ceded the family farm to him.

He seems to have been a bright youngster at school with, prophetically, religion as one of his 'very good' subjects. As a young man he was something of a wild card, enjoying his drink and dance and game of cards. He liked to 'cut a dash' as, for instance, being the first Radegundian motorcyclist. He was in the parish Passion play of 1930 as a soldier, quite ironically in the light of future events.

But a new lifestyle was emerging and was especially evident after his marriage. The 'new Franz' read religion-related matter, sang hymns at work and abstained from gambling. He became a daily communicant, fasting, it is said, until noon in reverence for the sacrament he had received. He became parish sacristan – and a strict one too: no chit-chat in the sacristy!

Part and parcel of his new-found faith was his total opposition to Nazism. He saw it as essentially anti-Christian. In March 1938 German troops occupied Austria and Hitler proclaimed Austria part of Germany. On 10 April Austrians voted *'Ja'* overwhelmingly to the *fait accompli* in a plebiscite of all 'Greater Germany'. Franz voted against; whether by *'Nein'* or spoiled vote is not certain. His boycott of the regime in one way or another included his refusal to give the greeting 'Heil Hitler'. And so to the crucial question of his life: could he in conscience serve in Hitler's army?

His conscience strongly said 'no'. In a remarkable series of private papers, which might be called 'the conscience of Franz Jägerstätter', he expressed his thoughts on military service and related issues. He believed that the German State and the Nazi party had become one entity, that in the circumstances of the time it was impossible to fight for the German State without fighting for 'the worst and most dangerous anti-Christian power that ever existed,' and that just as Hitler demanded public loyalty from his followers, so Christ demanded public loyalty from Christians.

He made no secret of his intention to refuse military service. Neighbours and relatives, priests and the bishop of Linz urged him to change his mind – but to no avail. There were those who thought his stance the crowning extreme of an over-religious life – or a sign of being slightly 'unhinged'.

In late February 1943 he received his summons to enlist. On 1 March he formally refused to serve. After imprisonment at Linz he was transferred to Tegel, Berlin. There both the chaplain and lawyer assigned to him failed to dent his resolve. Having accepted his 'no', the chaplain consoled him with the story of Franz Reineisch, a priest of the Pallotine order, who had persevered in a similar stand. At the chaplain's request he wrote a statement of his position in which he spoke of 'the community of saints and the community of the Nazi people,' of personal responsibility and divine judgement and promises. It can be considered his last spiritual testament.

The lawyer said that just before the trial, at his request, the officer-judges urged the prisoner to reconsider his decision. The answer was still no. The trial then took place and the mandatory sentence of death was pronounced. On the lawyer's initiative, Franz's wife and parish priest came to Berlin to plead for a change of mind before the sentence was confirmed. Again the answer was no.

On 9 August 1943, he wrote home for the last time. The letter ends with a quotation from a hymn or prayer to Our Lady: *'Maria mit dem Kinde lieb/uns noch allen Deinen Segen gieb'* ('Mary with the beloved Child, give us all your blessings'). He was executed that afternoon.

THE MAN WHO SAID NO

Seize the day and have your dream
Passion play and sword of wood
dance and sing that life is good
and then – another theme.

Frau und Kinder: happiness
plough the land and meet the Lord
Passion: speak the lonely word
a 'no' that is a 'yes'.

ENVOY EXTRAORDINARY

EDEL QUINN

'I would like you to remember always, whatever happens, that I am *glad* that you gave me the opportunity of going. I realise it is a privilege and also that, had you not persisted, I would never have been sent ... I am glad you let me go.' The addressee of the letter was Frank Duff, founder of the Legion of Mary. The writer was Edel Quinn, at the time of writing on her way to Africa as a Legion envoy.

She was born on 14 September 1907, the child of Charles and Louise (Burke Browne) Quinn. Her first home was at Greenane, near Kanturk, County Cork, where her father worked in a bank. There was a sequence of homes and schools as he was transferred from one bank to another. She was good at studies and sport, played the piano and loved to dance, and was noted for her gaiety and kindness.

In 1924 the family settled in Monkstown, County Dublin. Edel took a secretarial job. Her employer, a young French man, fell in love with her and proposed marriage. She gently explained that she had promised herself to God as a Poor Clare. To him we owe the precious 'Letters to Pierre', which she wrote to him after his departure from Ireland. The wife-that-never-was, who had helped to bring him back to the sacraments, became a private saint to him: he and his wife named one of their children after her. There was already a good deal of the Poor Clare in her, especially in her practice of 'doing without' and in her deep devotion to the Blessed Eucharist.

'I can't go on Thursday,' a friend said when Edel asked her to visit the family that day, 'I have a Legion of Mary meeting on Thursday.' 'Let me come', Edel replied. She came and saw and was conquered, becoming a member of the praesidium (which, interestingly enough, met quite near where Matt Talbot had collapsed and died). Frank Duff made her president of a praesidium for the rescue and rehabilitation of prostitutes. She became a legend of love to them; her rapport with these women whose background was so different to her own was quite astonishing.

Arrangements for her to join the Belfast Poor Clares were in motion when she fell ill. The diagnosis was advanced tuberculosis. The treatment was complete hospital rest. After a long stay in a sanatorium she left, feeling that it was not doing her any good and was a family financial burden and that she could be treated at home and could be 'doing something'.

This, of course, meant the Legion. She thought of Wales as a mission field. Frank Duff asked her to assist the Legion envoy in South Africa. She agreed. Then she was asked to be envoy in Central and East Africa. She agreed to this also. There were misgivings and protests because of her frail health. Her letter to Frank Duff indicates that his influence was decisive in having her appointed (and her own intervention must have moved many). She sailed for Africa in October 1936.

The work entailed encountering a culture hitherto unknown to her, explaining the Legion to missionaries and layfolk, training new members and coping with racial diversity. There were long journeys on atrocious roads (mostly in a two-seater Ford she called her 'Rolls Royce') and the trials of tropical climate. People warmed to this patient, courteous, good-humoured and hardworking woman. It was hard not to like her or to refuse her.

The work was eased by welcoming missionaries and responsive laity. A special boost was the recommendation of the Legion to the clergy by Monsignor Riberi, Apostolic Delegate to Equatorial Africa. It was his experience of the Legion in Africa that led him years later as internuncio to China to promote the Legion there, thus helping to prepare the Church for life in the communist regime, to initiate an epic chapter in the history of the Legion and in the religious history of the most populous nation on earth. We can claim a providential link between China-cum-Church-cum-Legion and Edel Quinn.

Nairobi, Mombasa, Nakuru, Kisumu, Kampala, Kilimanjaro, Zanzibar, Dar es Salaam, Mauritius, Lilongwe ... names like these added a new music to the Legion gazetteer and illustrate the immensity of her mission. In these and many other places she established the Legion as a dynamic part of the local Church. And this 'new and delightful thing: African people cooperating in the work of evangelisation' (to quote the Legion journal) was the achievement of a young woman on the edge of grave illness.

She was also, of course, a woman of deep spiritual resources. She told a colleague that Mass, Communion, the gospel and the de Montfort doctrine of utter dedication to Our Lady were the vital forces in her life (she could have added the influence of Saint Thérèse of Lisieux) and that Communion gave her the strength for the most difficult tasks; to be deprived of it was her greatest hardship.

She put a special value on time. Her words about that mysterious reality are memorable: 'The saints never lost time. Live for the day. Our eternity is built on time. Why lose a moment on the way during a brief journey? Only one life, and perhaps only a short part of it, in which to prove our love'.

By April 1937 she had the Legion well organised in the Nairobi area. She then moved to Mombasa and Kilimanjaro, including points between, and on to Kisumu and Zanzibar and back to Kenya. She worked in Uganda and Tanganyika (now the mainland and major part of Tanzania). She travelled across the Indian Ocean to Mauritius and back to Africa to Nyasaland (now Malawi), and it was there in 1941 that tuberculosis took over again.

After nearly two years in hospitals in South Africa, she returned to Nairobi and resumed work at an incredible tempo, considering her state of health. In April 1944 she collapsed. She died in the Convent of the Precious Blood in Nairobi on the evening of 12 May. Her remains rest in the missionaries' cemetery, Msongari, Nairobi.

ENVOY EXTRAORDINARY

Cot in Greenane, grave in Nairobi earth
so much between: young man trés plein d'amour
sacraments, prayer, desire to be cloistered, poor
tennis and typing, street-girls and pain and mirth
minarets, missions, villages, dust and drums
black and brown fingers moving the rosary beads
African voices telling of lovely deeds
– all for a Lady, all for the One who comes

Convent room and setting sun
Magnificat: assignment done.

EL CORDERITO

ALFIE LAMBE

A young man of twenty wrote a letter from his heart. Whether he realised it or not, it was the most important letter of his life: the acceptance of a special Legion of Mary mission in South America: 'Need I say that I am unworthy and completely unable to carry out such work? For that very reason I wish very much to be allowed to do the work and because I know that God will receive great glory from my efforts.'

Alphonsus Lambe came from Tullamore in the Irish midlands and was born on 24 June 1932. He had a great desire to be a Christian Brother but after a short time with them he had to leave because of his frail health. Membership of the Tullamore praesidium of the Legion of Mary helped him to overcome his disappointment and enhanced his already deep devotion to Our Lady, making it a focus for apostolate.

His mentor in the praesidium, Tom Crowley, recommended him to Séamus Grace, who was initiating and directing a system of Legion extension in rural Ireland. Alfie joined him in this, especially after the closure of the firm that employed him left him more time for Legion service. He worked mainly in Counties Mayo, Kerry and Cavan. His letters to Séamus reveal the ups and downs of the enterprise and his utter fidelity to duty. His diary reveals the prayerful background of his work.

He had the gift of 'converting' those who were unfavourable to the Legion. A famous example of this involved his cycling ten miles only to get a 'no' from a Kerry parish priest, cycling back to base (both journeys in the pouring rain) and reappearing the next morning. The impressed priest decided that, whatever about the rain, Alfie represented 'pennies from heaven' and changed his 'no' to 'yes'.

Frank Duff, founder of the Legion and a gifted talent-spotter in matters apostolic, thought of him as a companion to Séamus Grace, who was earmarked for South America. And so to the momentous letter and his departure on 16 July 1953 (Feast of Our Lady of Mount Carmel).

His South American work had much in common with his previous work in Ireland, but the milieu and atmosphere were very different. In cinematic terms it was like changing from standard screen black and white to wide screen full colour, with bishops, nuncios, cardinals and the occasional politician joining the cast – a cast of thousands racially and socially varied, basically Catholic influenced by spiritism and superstition. Heady stuff, we could say, for someone just out of his teens, but the young Tullamorian kept his head and focused on his essential mission.

In Colombia he worked both 'in the field' with Séamus Grace and Joaquina Lucas, an experienced envoy from the Philippines, and at learning Spanish. Then he was called to Legionless Ecuador. Bishop Echeverria of Ambato, who had asked for an envoy, became his staunch friend and liaison with his brother bishops. Progress was spectacular. All the bishops except one admitted the Legion into their dioceses. Praesidia of Hispanics, Indians, as well as prisoners and sufferers from leprosy were set up. He was the moving spirit of the publication in Quito of a Spanish edition with a South American supplement of the Legion periodical *Maria Legionis*.

Ecuador's Cardinal De La Torre invited him to accompany him to the International Eucharistic Congress in Rio de Janeiro in 1955. On the way he promoted the Legion in Peru and Bolivia. In Rio he buttonholed more bishops than he could count. In southern Brazil he helped the newly arrived envoy Mary Clerkin. And then, on instructions from Dublin, he went further south to Argentina to face the biggest challenge of his mission.

In Legion terms Argentina was an almost untouched land. The Legion existed in only one diocese and in a few religious houses. As regards lay apostolate, the bishops favoured 'official' Catholic action. There had just been a revolution; perhaps it was not the best time to introduce new religious movements. The Lambe charm and gift of persuasion had to work overtime. The second largest country in South America made huge demands of distance on the Lambe body, which was not in the best of health.

In time the bishops yielded to Don Alfonso El Corderito (the Little Lamb), as he had come to be called – the names expressing Hispanic courtesy and affection respectively. The most important and most resistant citadel to fall was the Archdiocese of Buenos Aires, which covered the centre of that vast city. Perhaps the most important praesidium he ever founded was that in the university, which was a communist stronghold. There were threatening phone calls and calls for his deportation. His most 'prophetic' praesidium was that of Syrian members (all men) of the Orthodox Church. Pre-Vatican II ecumenism! (By this time he was dreaming of going to communist-ruled Russia.) There were forays to Paraguay and Uraguay and return visits to Peru and Bolivia.

In December 1958 he collapsed. A stomach ulcer was detected. But far worse was soon discovered: inoperable lymphosarcoma. He died on 21 January, Feast of Saint Agnes ('The Lamb'), in 1959. He was interred in the cemetery of the Christian Brothers (the order he had once hoped to join) in Buenos Aires.

The notes of his last retreat five months before reveal the mind and heart of this remarkable young man who is one of the 'greats' of the Church in twentieth-century South America: he commits himself to what he was surely doing already: daily Mass, Communion, Rosary – all in union with Our Lady.

He had written to his mother: 'I love every city and pueblo that I enter, I am at home under every sky ... There is no one in the world richer than I, there is no one in the world poorer than I.' Saint Francis of Assisi could have written that: 'El Corderito' echoing 'Il Poverello'.

EL CORDERITO

Lambs are timid: this particular one
goes into battle, braveheart through and through
lambs cling to dams: he has his Mother too
joyful to be her son

Lambs stay at home: he goes from land to land
saying the word, doing the lovely deed
like Francis bringing hope to deep-down need
all by royal command

Lamb of God, the Crucified enthroned
who said, 'My lambs know me and I know mine'
feast of Agnes, nineteen fifty-nine
this lamb goes home.

THE GOOD FATHER

JOHN XXIII

The elderly man had been a diarist since his young days and 28 October 1958 certainly deserved an entry: 'Feast of the Holy Apostles Simon and Jude. Holy Mass in the Mathilde Chapel ... On the eleventh ballot I was elected Pope.'

Angelo Giuseppe Roncalli was born and christened on 25 November 1881 in Sotto il Monte near Bergamo in northern Italy. The Roncallis were peasant farmers, sharing their crops with their landlord, sharing too with those poorer than themselves. He grew up in a milieu in which hardship and faith were taken for granted. In his early years his mentor was his grand-uncle and godfather Xaverio. Later he drew near to the parish priest, Father Rebuzzini, who coached him for entry into the junior seminary at Bergamo. After the seminary came the Roman College in Rome, where his studies were interrupted by military service, which was a rude awakening for the sheltered seminarian. He was ordained priest in 1904.

He became secretary to Bishop Radini-Tedeschi of Bergamo and also professor of Church history in the diocesan seminary. He hero-worshipped his dynamic bishop and wrote a book about him. Another hero of his was Cardinal Andrea Carlo Ferrari of Milan, whose beatification he was to promote when Pope.

He was back in the army in the First World War as a hospital orderly and chaplain. It was a harrowing and learning experience, giving him a detestation of war and an appreciation of the men he served, most of them peasants like himself. His chaplaincy over, he destroyed his uniform; perhaps it was too stark a reminder of horror and death.

After some youth work, in 1921 he became National Director of the Propagation of the Faith. In 1924 he began an enduring friendship with Giovanni Battista Montini, who was to succeed him as Paul VI, and preached a sermon in which he revealed his reservations about the ruling Fascists of Mussolini and his liking for the Italian People's Party (the predecessors of the Christian Democrats).

Probably as a result of the sermon (an embarrassed Holy See moving towards rapprochement with the Italian State and an angry Mussolini demanding his removal from Italy) he found himself appointed apostolic visitor to Bulgaria. With the appointment went episcopal ordination and the beginning of a long acquaintance with the world's most famous train, the Orient Express.

He endeared himself to the tiny Catholic population in Bulgaria of both Slav and Latin rite: they called him *'Diado'* (Good Father). He also tried to endear the Catholic Church to the Orthodox Church which became a type of apprenticeship in ecumenism. The 'visit' lasted until 1935 when he became apostolic delegate to Turkey with responsibility also for Greece. In Turkey he saw a secular state in the making under Kemal Ataturk. In Greece he met a society in which 'Greek' was virtually 'Orthodox' and 'Vatican' and 'ecumenism' were politically incorrect words.

He watched the Second World War mainly from Istanbul. He helped to relieve famine in Greece. An important work of his was tracing prisoners of war. Another was saving Jews from the Nazis. In this his ally was Franz von Papen, the (Catholic) German ambassador to neutral Turkey. (When von Papen was on trial in Nuremberg charged with war crimes, the former apostolic delegate wrote an unsolicited letter to the president of the tribunal to say that 'he gave me the chance to save the lives of 24,000 Jews'. The letter may have saved von Papen's life. Years later von Papen returned the compliment by testifying at John's beatification process to his work for the Jews.)

And then suddenly and unexpectedly to Paris as nuncio to post-war France. It was a difficult mission: a nation emerging from enemy occupation; the new concept of 'worker priests'; and the question of removing bishops rated pro-Vichy by the De Gaulle government. He studied French Catholicism and pondered Cardinal Archbishop Suhard's vision of a Church more 'alive' to the modern world.

In 1953 he was created cardinal and made patriarch of Venice; some direct pastoral work after so many years of diplomacy. He was concerned about the Venetian poor and unemployed. He seems to have had a 'soft spot' for gondoliers (they had escorted him in style in his ceremonial arrival), presenting the prizes at their annual regatta. He tried to be all things to all politicians. His pastorate in Venice can been seen in hindsight as a 'dry run' of his papacy.

Pope Pius XII died on 9 October 1958. The conclave to elect his successor met on 25 October. Angelo Roncalli had lived under five popes. By midday on 28 October he realised that he would be the next. He took the name John, he said, because it was the name of the two men in the gospels closest to Christ and because it stood for love; partly too, as he told a French cardinal, in memory of John XXII, who had lived at Avignon.

The fat man with the friendly face, who clearly liked to meet people and who clearly was not going to be 'the prisoner of the Vatican', became a refreshing part of world news. He soon showed that he was not the 'caretaker Pope' that many were expecting. On 25 January 1959 he announced the most momentous decision of his pontificate: to convoke a General Council for the renewal and *aggiornamento* (updating) of the Church and the promotion of Christian unity.

Between that announcement and the opening of the Council came his encyclical on the social order, *Mater et Magistra* (Mother and Teacher). In it he showed great concern for rural people, surely a reflection of his own experience in Sotto il Monte and a tribute to the sort of people he came from.

The Second Vatican Council opened on 11 October 1962. John gave what has been called 'the speech of his life'. He had an immediate audience of about three thousand bishops (the largest gathering of bishops in the history of the Church) and of millions more on radio and television. The speech reflected his life experience, historical training and deep faith, and echoed voices like those of Radini-Tedeschi and Suhard:

> Christ is the central reality of human history and life. The essential faith is to be treasured and guarded and presented pastorally with a sense of its importance to the modern

world. It enlightens people as to their nature and destiny. The Church esteems and assesses the achievements of the human genius. The Church is duty-bound to promote the unity of Christians that Christ so ardently prayed for. The Council helps towards that unity of the human family which will be the foundation of a heaven-like earthly society. The Council will help the Church to look fearlessly ahead.

Some found John a breath of fresh air, others found him a dangerous draught. By the end of the first session, the Council was getting on course in the Joannine wind.

His last eight months were quite remarkable. Shortly before the council opened, medical procedures revealed advanced cancer. His part in the defusing of the Cuban missile crisis (October 1962), his receiving in audience the daughter and son-in-law of the Soviet leader Khrushchev (March 1963), the issuing of his great encyclical *Peace on Earth* (April 1963), acclaimed by the United Nations and the Council itself – all this and more was on the agenda of a dying man in his eighties.

On 17 May 1963, he said his last Mass and on 31 May he received viaticum and the sacrament of the sick. On 3 June he said twice with great emphasis Peter's words to the risen Christ: 'Lord, you know that I love you'. He died that evening.

> *Look ahead ... there's also memory*
> *did you look back in nineteen sixty three?*
> *so many people, places, happenings*
> *parents, peasants, priests, and popes and kings*
> *soldiers, gondoliers, the rich, the poor*
> *those with faith, without it, those unsure*
> *Lombardy pines, Bosphorus minarets*
> *Paris, Venice, Orient Express*
> *Council, unity, Church on the move*
> *all for the One who knows he has your love*
> *truly an Angelo straight from the Lord*
> *thanks, good-bye, dear John the twenty-third.*

GRATEFULLY AND HOPEFULLY YOURS

G.K. CHESTERTON AND C.S. LEWIS

G.K. Chesterton

In 1908 a well-known Fleet Street journalist, whose rotund figure with sombrero, swordstick and cape was a famous feature of 'the Street', published a book about the Christian faith. Gilbert Keith Chesterton (1874–1936), influenced by the milieu he moved in, had become something of a pagan and pantheist. Yet he grew increasingly critical of the 'creeds' of that milieu and frightened of the 'abyss' and 'extreme evil' which he thought at least part of it was leading to. He studied the Christian faith he had largely abandoned and concluded that it made a great deal of sense of human life and experience. And so to 'Orthodoxy' and his debut as a Christian apologist.

He became a Catholic in 1922 'to get rid of my sins', as he put it. In his pre-Orthodoxy days he had 'hung on to the remains of religion by one thin thread of gratitude ... I thanked whatever gods there might be ... with a sort of mystical minimum of gratitude.'

Catholicism confirmed and enriched this mindset. 'These doctrines [of the Church] seem to me to link up my whole life ... they especially affect ... the chief idea of my life ... of taking things with gratitude and not taking things for granted ... I find myself ratified in the realisation of the miracle of being alive.' Catholicism helped him to uncover 'the submerged sunrise of wonder' (which can evoke gratitude) that was hidden 'at the back of our brains'. He found in the Church the happy ending to what he called his 'romance of receptiveness'. He was especially impressed by the sacrament of penance whereby sin ('perhaps most horrible to me because it is ingratitude') is got rid of and the penitent 'may be grey and gouty but he is only five minutes old.'

In 1925 he published his epic book, *The Everlasting Man*: a panoramic treatment of 'The Creature called Man' and 'The Man called Christ', centred on the Christ of the gospels. Other books on religious subjects included biographies of Saint Francis of Assisi, who wrote, he said, the grammar of acceptance and gratitude, and Saint Thomas Aquinas, whose realist philosophy appealed to him. He was an incredibly prolific writer – poems, novels, detective stories, essays, biographies, plays – and a well-known lecturer and broadcaster.

He proclaimed with gratitude the wonder of the ordinary. For him small was beautiful. He loved England but disliked its having an empire. A London 'village' like Kensington or Notting Hill meant more to him than London as a whole. A family business was preferable to a capitalist conglomerate. In his *G.K.'s Weekly* he espoused small-scale ownership (distributism) against big business and State socialism. The core of his social thought was the family.

He had a gift for pithily expressing the heart of his subject matter, often in paradox. He combined faith and reason in a way reminiscent of Saint Thomas Aquinas. Perhaps it was this that made Etienne Gilson, a great authority on Thomas, say that Chesterton was 'one of the greatest thinkers who ever existed'; he had been stunned by the Aquinas biography.

He had a special regard for Ireland and he was in Dublin for the Eucharistic Congress in 1932. His record of it is the lyrical and perceptive *Christendom in Dublin*.

In their telegram of sympathy and tribute on the occasion of his death in 1936, Pope Pius XI and his Secretary of State (the future Pius XII) called him 'Defender of the Catholic Faith'. They could also have named him 'Apostle of Gratitude'.

> *Knight with swordstick but no sword*
> *fighting with word on word on word*
> *doing homage to King and Lord*
> *in gratitude to One adored*

> *At last his voice no longer stirred*
> *I like to think that then he heard*
> *another voice, a welcoming Word*
> *saying, 'Thank you, come aboard'.*

C.S. Lewis

One of those who acknowledged their debt to Chesterton was an Ulsterman temperamentally like him and similarly talented: Clive Staples Lewis (1898–1963). He was born in Belfast but spent most of his life in England, mainly at Oxford where he was a student, lecturer, fellow and tutor, and also at Cambridge where he had the Chair of Medieval and Renaissance English. He was reared an Anglican, lost his faith to become an atheist and then returned first to belief in God and then to belief in Christianity. (For further detail on this see Lewis' autobiography, *Surprised by Joy*.)

With a literary style that ranged from the colloquial to the poetic, he became perhaps the most famous Christian apologist of the century. His best known book is *The Screwtape Letters*, a profound and witty treatment of temptation and human nature (and also diabolic nature) from the satanic viewpoint. The trilogy *Out of the Silent Planet, Perelandra (Voyage to Venus)* and *That Hideous Strength* deals imaginatively with the struggle between good and evil, between God and Satan (with the enemies of God seen also, as in the *Spiritual Exercises* of Saint Ignatius Loyola, as the enemies of humankind).

The Chronicles of Narnia, a series of children's books, is shot through with Christian meaning and imagery. Spoken pieces, including broadcast talks, also became books. Much of his material was published post-humously. His fame led to what must have been a taxing correspondence which he conducted with courtesy and patience. He never became a Catholic but there is much of 'the Catholic' in his thinking.

He was a great believer in heaven, seeing it as God's response to our deepest longings, as fully lighted reality after our 'shadowlands'. His sermon-essay, *The Weight of Glory*, is a classic. Heaven is the theme of the finale to the last *Narnia* book and of the last chapter of his final book, *Letters to Malcolm*, a chapter that can serve as his farewell spiritual testament.

Perelandra, Narnia, Aslan
parables of a Lover's cosmic plan
human weakness, devil's brew
subjected to analysis
for telling us all this, thanks, C.S.

Out of the pit of atheistic night
into the shadowlands that lead to light
where all our longing is fulfilled
and fear is killed in utter bliss
for telling us all this, thanks, C.S.

Surprised by Joy? Oh yes, C.S.

THE VIRTUOUS ONE

GLADYS AYLWARD

A newly arrived parlourmaid in her room in the elegant London house looked at her Bible and shillings and pence and prayed: 'God, here's me, here's my Bible, here's my money. Use us!'

Gladys Aylward (1902–1970) came from Edmonton, Middlesex, of a working-class and strongly Christian family. After some schooling she worked mainly as a parlourmaid in London West End houses. But her thoughts strayed far beyond her 'upstairs-downstairs' surroundings and focused on one dream: to be a missionary in China.

She enrolled at a mission centre where prospective missionaries were trained, but she was hopeless at studying, so had to leave. She worked in Welsh slums and nearly died of pneumonia. She returned to Edmonton to convalesce with China, apparently receding fast. Then she heard of the elderly Jeannie Lawson running a one-woman mission in Yangcheng, Shansi, in northern China, who was looking for a helper and successor. China ceased to retreat.

However, she had to find her fare and so she came to the big house and the small room in Kensington where she uttered the famous prayer quoted above. Week by week she saved every available shilling until she reached the magic sum of forty-seven pounds and ten shillings, with which she bought a London to Tientsin ticket, mainly on the Trans-Siberian Railway. She left London in October 1932 complete with tinned food, traveller's cheque, Bible and much trust in God. She travelled right across the Euro-Asian landmass from The Hague to Vladivostok, through Japan, Tientsin (China at last!) and on to Peking, Tsechow and Yangcheng. The 'London Sparrow', as she was afterwards called, had flown eight thousand miles by train, ship and mule.

Yangcheng was an ancient city on an important trade route – it was a place of inns. Jeannie and Gladys opened their inn and gave it a name straight out of the Gospel of Matthew: 'The Inn of the

Eight Happinesses'. With board and lodging their clientele of muleteers and carriers received as a 'bonus' an introduction to Jesus Christ by way of Bible stories.

After Jeannie's death Gladys soldiered on. The local mandarin made her enforcement officer of the prohibition of the immemorial foot-binding of little girls. She combined foot inspections with gospel preaching and forming of Christian communities. She brought a new spirit and hope, especially to women. She became a mother figure to orphan children. The people called her 'Ai-weh-deh', the nearest they could get to 'Aylward'; appropriately it meant 'The Virtuous One'.

She spoke five dialects and in 1936 became a Chinese citizen; she felt at home with 'my people', as she called them. A special example of this relationship was the friendship, based on mutual respect, between the ex-parlourmaid of Kensington, a Christian missionary, and the Yangcheng mandarin, the embodiment of the ancient Confucian culture of China; it was one of the great friendships in East-West history.

They met at a time when Confucian China to some extent was confused China; it was a time of regional warlords, the central nationalist government of Chiang Kai Chek, the communist movement of Mao Tse-tung, the invading Japanese and all those who dreamt of an imperial comeback. War came to Shansi and the Japanese briefly occupied Yangcheng. Life for Gladys now involved not only routine mission work but caring for victims of conflict, commuting between nationalist-held and Japanese-held areas.

Then in the spring of 1940 came her most famous achievement: her shepherding of nearly one hundred children from Yangcheng across the mountains and the Yellow River south-west to Sian in nationalist-held territory. It was a month's journey of two to three hundred miles with little food and much faith. The epic trek was hardly over when she collapsed and nearly died. She then moved to a mission where she cared for leprosy patients. She returned to England in 1949, the year of the Communist takeover in China.

Even so, as with Francis Xavier, her heart was towards eastern horizons. She spent most of the rest of her life in Taiwan, where she died on 1 January 1970. Her grave in Taipei looks towards mainland China where she had once written: 'Do not wish me out of this or in any way seek to get me out for I will not be got out while this trial is on. These are my people, God has given them to me and I will live or die with them for Him and His Glory'.

China cups in Kensington
Chinese vases – treat with care
counting shillings one by one
adding up to get a fare

Inn where God's events are told
pupils in a gentle school
mandarin in cloth of gold
culture by a lotus pool

Songs of praise and battle screams
surge of faith and tide of war
children crossing hills and stream
following her who found her star

Island home: still say the word
pray and hope and care and bless
new year: time to meet the Lord
share his eight-fold happiness.

THE MAN OF THREE WISHES

JOHN BRADBURNE

One day in 1942, halfway through the Second World War, an officer of the Indian army, recently arrived in north India, brought a record of light music to another officer who had a gramophone. The latter put the record aside and said, 'We'll play Bach instead'. So began the life-long friendship between John Dove and John Bradburne. Little did the light music man dream that he would come to regard the Bach man as a saint and would later write his biography.

John Bradburne came from Cumbria in north-west England, the son of a minister of the Church of England. After a public school education and a stint at Cambridge he joined the Indian army and saw service in Malaya, India and Burma. However, he was occupied with more than the war. Various factors combined in him to evoke a search, a longing, sometimes confused and uncertain, for God.

In 1947 he was received into the Catholic Church at the Benedictine abbey of Buckfast in Devon, but his hopes of joining them came to nothing. After two stints as stoker on coastal craft (meant as a measure of self-sorting out) and still cloister-minded, he became a working guest of the Carthusians at Parkminster in Sussex. A Jew was being received there into the Church and this heightened his desire to devote himself to the conversion of the Jews. He managed to reach Jerusalem to stay there with Our Lady's Fathers of Sion (a congregation founded for that purpose) and afterwards he spent eighteen months with them at Louvain in Belgium.

He was then on the road to Palestine again, getting as far as Palma in southern Italy where he assisted the parish priest and became a local 'character'. The highlight of his time there was his promise to 'Miriam' (his name for Our Lady) not to marry but to serve her and her Son in celibacy – his 'marriage' to her, as he called it. Back then to England for a varied sequence of events and occupations, including his last attempt to join a religious order (the Benedictines of Prinknash in Gloucestershire).

Next stop: Africa. Through the good offices of John Dove (by now a priest in the Society of Jesus and working in what is now Zimbabwe) and of the Franciscans (of whose Third Order he was a member) he became a rather unusual lay missionary: working at this and that, writing his poetry, playing his music, delighting in nature (with a special fondness for eagles and bees) and, of course, praying a lot – he was devoted to the Blessed Trinity, the Blessed Sacrament and Miriam/Mary/Morning Star. And so, after a visit to England and Palestine, to the defining phase of his life: Mutemwa.

On his arrival in the then Southern Rhodesia in 1962, John Bradburne had said that he had three wishes. The first was to live with and serve those afflicted with leprosy. At Mutemwa there were about a hundred of them. Those seeking to better their condition asked John to be their warden. The answer was of course yes. To him every patient was a precious person. His service of them was humble and detailed, very much 'hands on'. He had a decent chapel built for them and helped at Mass and Communion. Some of his most moving poems are about them. A favourite text of his regarding them was Philippians 3:21: 'The Lord Jesus Christ will transform our wretched bodies into likenesses of his own glorious body.'

At first he was supported by a small committee, 'the Friends of Mutemwa'. But then he clashed with the 'national' committee that succeeded them. They found him defective in bookkeeping (which indeed was not his forte) and over-generous in provisioning. He found them impersonal and cheese-paring towards the patients. Sacked and banished almost completely from the premises, he managed to maintain a limited presence and was eventually allowed back but not as warden. His 'committee ordeal' was the beginning of the fulfilment of his second wish: to die a martyr.

By this time a guerrilla war was waging between the minority white government of Ian Smith and those who wanted a majority-ruled Zimbabwe. One atrocity during the war was the murder of four Dominican sisters and three Jesuits at Musami mission by persons still not definitely known. Two of the Jesuits, Father Christopher Shepherd-Smith from Kenya and Brother John Conway from Ireland, were friends of his. Another tragedy for him was the fatal shooting at a checkpoint of Doctor Luisa Giudotti, a helper at Mutemwa.

On the night of 3/4 September 1979, John Dove, on leave in Ireland, had a compelling consciousness of someone in agony. The agony was John Bradburne's. According to informants he was abducted by *mujhibas* (youngsters who assisted the guerrillas) and brought by night to the headquarters of a guerrilla commander. The commander treated him with respect and, though advised that releasing him would be a security risk, finally told him that he was free to go. He set off with a party which included two guerrillas. On the morning of 5 September his bullet-riddled body was found on a road some miles from Mutemwa. His second wish had been granted.

His third wish was to be buried in the Franciscan habit. At the funeral Mass three lilies were placed on the coffin in token of his devotion to the Blessed Trinity. Drops of blood were seen to fall from it. The body and coffin were examined but no seepage or dampness or blood was observed. And there was no Franciscan habit. The oversight was soon remedied. On 12 September 1979 in Chishawasha Mission cemetery John Bradburne's third wish came true.

Man of three wishes, man of the Blessed Three
Miriam's champion, knight of the King her Son
Philippians wonder-text: three, twenty-one
cripples will walk again, the blind will see

On pilgrim way: the shadowlands, the night
Zimbabwe road: Emmaus: into light.

GOSPEL RADICAL

DOROTHY DAY

One day in 1927 a nun was walking near her convent in Staten Island near New York when a young woman came up to her and asked her how she should go about having her baby daughter baptised. Sister Aloysia became interested in the mother as well as the baby. Within a year the baby was baptised and the mother received into the Church.

Dorothy Day (1897–1980) was brought up in Brooklyn, New York, Oakland, near San Francisco and Chicago. Her father was a newspaper man. She felt drawn towards the poor and underprivileged. She made the Chicago meat industry scenes of Upton Sinclair's novel *The Jungle* real to her by exploring them. She discovered writers like Tolstoi and especially Dostoyevski. By 1927 she could look back over a decade or so of left-wing journalism, trouble with the law, brief civil marriage and life with Forster Batterham on Staten Island.

She seemed an unlikely candidate for Catholicism. But there were influences and stirrings: the good example of Catholic girls she knew and Our Lady edging in through the gift of rosary beads (given to her by a communist room mate), the attraction of Mass and the fact that where she had lived, the Catholic Church in its broad membership was the Church of the poor. (In a pre-Catholic way, Anglican worship, it seems, had given her a sense of God as the source of the beauty of the world. And, of course, there was the spell of Dostoyevski with his Christian insight.) She parted traumatically from Batterham, who was not interested in religion or marriage, and was received into the Church; an event, as she recalled in later life, quite devoid of comfortable feelings.

The Wall Street crash of 1929 ushered in grave economic depression with more and more people jobless and homeless. Dorothy's faith was strong but she was disappointed at the lack of social radicalism in the Church. She prayed for guidance. The answer to her prayer arrived in the shape of Peter Maurin.

This middle-aged Frenchman was a sort of twentieth-century Francis of Assisi, living an almost moneyless life. He had a vision of a radical Christian social order, 'in which it would be easier for people to be good'. For this, he told Dorothy, a socially radical paper or journal was necessary. Thus, *The Catholic Worker* was born in Times Square, New York, in 1933 on 1 May, Labour Day, traditionally celebrated by socialists and communists. The paper caught on and the print order soared. Dorothy was editor, writing in a person-to-person 'at home' style. Peter expounded his message in poetic and repetitive 'Easy Essays'.

One of his main themes was hospitality to the homeless in keeping with Matthew 25:35-45 (his and Dorothy's tessera). Every parish should have its 'house of hospitality', every home its 'Christroom'. Dorothy set a good example in her own apartment. By 1936 there were over thirty such houses in the United States where the poor were welcomed without charge.

Less successful were the farming communities that the movement set up in response to Peter's dream of Christians lovingly together on God's good earth – the earth was good but the togetherness proved tough. Things went better for those Catholic Worker families who settled on the land in a more traditional way.

Peter died in 1949 and Dorothy continued as 'mother' of the Catholic Worker movement. She became, according to the Jesuit *America* in its special issue on her in 1972, the person who best represented 'the aspiration and action of the American Catholic community'. She went against the aforesaid community by refusing to support Franco in the Spanish Civil War in the 1930s. Several bishops banned *The Catholic Worker* from churches and schools with the consequent drop of circulation. She went against many in the movement itself by her pacifist stance in the Second World War. In the 1950s she shared in the vexations of the anti-communist campaign, got into trouble regarding civil defence regulations and experienced a taste of racist terror in Georgia.

The 1960s could be called her 'Rome' decade. She was one of the 'Mothers of Peace', thanking John XXIII for his encyclical on peace and asking for a radical condemnation of modern tools of war. She was in a group praying and fasting for a Vatican Council statement favouring conscientious objectors and the non-violent way to social justice and condemning weapons of mass destruction. The Council obliged just before it ended. She was a guest of honour at the International Congress of the Laity.

She opposed the Vietnam War, the war industry it generated and the horrific methods used in its prosecution, and supported draft-resisters. She also supported a man after her own heart because of his emphasis on religious values and non-violence: César Chavez, founder of a union in California fighting for exploited workers.

She was convinced of the importance of every individual and she hungered for a just social order. She prayed much and read much: her favourite author was Dostoyevski, who had helped so notably to mould her mind; a special moment for her in a visit to Russia in 1971 was to meditate and pray at his grave.

She spent her last few years in retirement but continued to write her piece for *The Catholic Worker*. She died on 29 November 1980. Her remains lie in Resurrection Cemetery on Staten Island, near where a young woman met a nun in 1927.

Her grave is near the ocean: endless sea
primeval, restless, still, a mystery
symbol of God, womb of humanity
of all who live and pray, aspire, endure
symbol of life and love, of all like her
whose hearts are wide and deep, who love the poor
know that what's done for them is done to Him
whose word is hope: 'God's with us, let's begin'
find in His Heart their peace and enter in.

PEOPLE OF THE PEARL

JANANI LUWUM AND COMPANIONS

Uganda is a country three times the size of Ireland with fertile soil, beautiful landscapes and a sunny climate, bordered by great mountains and lakes, the land of the fountains of the Nile – the Pearl of Africa, to give it its poetic name. Anglican and Catholic missionaries introduced Christianity to Uganda in the 1870s. In the 1880s both Anglican and Catholic Ugandans died in the persecution of the Kabaka Mwanga. (At his canonisation of the martyred Catholics, Pope Paul VI also praised the Anglicans who gave their lives for Christ.)

In the colonial share-out of Africa, Uganda fell to the British, who established a protectorate that lasted until 1962. The country became independent with the Kabaka as president and Milton Obote as prime minister. Five years later Obote abolished the kabakate with a certain Idi Amin as his right-hand man. In 1971, while Obote was absent at a Commonwealth conference, Amin seized power.

It soon became clear that the regime of 'Big Daddy' had little time for human rights and that the army had been given wide powers of arrest and execution. Amin came under pressure from Arab extremists and seemed to dream of muslimising Uganda. Out of the mix of tribalism, hatred, religious fanaticism, paranoia of power of Amin and his followers came a maelstrom of murders.

The murdered victims of the terror included: Clement Kiggundi and John Serwanika, priest-journalists whose writing angered the administration; Teresa Nanziri-Bukenya, a university warden, for refusing to give incriminating evidence against a student; six young actors who were to perform in a play honouring the Mwanga martyrs; and chief justice Benedict Kiwanuka for calling for a curb on army powers of arrest.

The man whose murder more than any other revealed to the outside world what was happening in Uganda was Janani Luwum. He grew up a bright youngster who absorbed all the education he could get and he became a teacher. The turning point of his life was a deep religious experience while he was a young man, which he dated precisely 12:30 on the afternoon of 6 January 1948. He was ordained in the Anglican ministry and became bishop of northern Uganda and then in 1974 leader of the Anglican community in the Pearl of Africa as Archbishop of Uganda. 'We must love the president,' said this gentle and charismatic man, 'we must pray for him. He is a child of God.' But 'the child of God' was keeping an eye on him, especially, no doubt, after he took part in a meeting of protest against the breakdown in the rule of law.

February 1977 was his month of drama and death. His house was searched for arms. Following a protest by the Anglican bishops concerning the excesses of the regime, he and other important people were summoned to a display of military might and of allegedly seized weapons. The proceedings included a mock trial in which he and his brother bishop Okuth (who had been under arrest for a short while) were accused of plotting against the government. Within hours of the display there were two radio announcements: that he and two cabinet ministers had been arrested and that all three had died in a car accident. His exhumed body revealed that he had been repeatedly shot.

With the help of Tanzanian troops, Obote resumed power in 1979. There was a new terror. One of its victims was Ponsiano Kafuuma. He was an active member of the Pioneer Total Abstinence Association, promoting the Pioneer ideal in the Diocese of Masaka. He was also on the management committee of the Masaka Cooperative Movement.

In September 1982 he was accused of collaboration with guerrillas and put on view as one. He died in custody only a few days after arrest. A priest-friend came on behalf of the family to take away the body. He was told that death had been natural but the body, with Rosary still around the neck, told of torture and murder.

He had told the priest of his concern about the state of his country: 'I know the path I have tried to walk all my life and with God's help I shall not leave it ... I love the truth and I love my country.' He was a true patriot of the Pearl of Africa.

PEOPLE OF THE PEARL

Deep flows the Nile with blood on foam
warm shines the sun on fields of fear
the warden, actors, priests who write
the bishop, judge, the Pioneer
soldiers of grace in freedom's fight
all known to God, to God most dear
clear speaks the Truth, warm shines the Light
deep flows the Love that brings them home.

CHAMPIONS OF THE POOR

OSCAR ROMERO AND COMPANIONS

On 26 February 1980 Radio Telefís Éireann broadcast a programme about El Salvador, which included an interview with Oscar Romero, Archbishop of San Salvador. A month later the man whose strong, broad face had filled the screen was murdered while saying Mass.

From the sixteenth to the nineteenth century what is now El Salvador was part of the vast Spanish colonial empire. It was here that the defiance of Spain in Central America began in 1811. After the collapse of the Central American Federation it continued as a separate state. In the course of time in the interests of what can be called 'coffee capitalism' (coffee farming being the country's main industry), a powerful land-owning class developed with tenant farmers and communal Indians becoming agricultural labourers.

Various groupings and influences characterised El Salvador in the 1970s: the tiny minority (the so-called 'Fourteen Families', though there were more than fourteen) that owned most of the land; the rural peasants; the urban workers and middle-class; the political parties; armed forces (official and unofficial); and the United States involvement.

He and his fellow bishop Rivera Damas issued a pastoral, in which they condemned the 'institutional violence' directed against the 'poor minority' and appealed for a social consensus on their behalf. Most El Salvadorean bishops thought him unwise in his stance and influenced by an undesirable form of liberation theology. In another pastoral he dealt with three 'idolatries': worship of wealth, of private property and of political power.

It was in the 1970s that Oscar Romero, a priest since 1942, became Auxiliary Bishop of San Salvador, moved to Santiago de Maria as its bishop and then returned to San Salvador as its archbishop. He was known as a dedicated pastor but hardly seen as a leader in the struggle for social justice. But shortly after his appointment as archbishop a friend of his, Rutilio Grande of the

Society of Jesus, a champion of the poor and a denouncer of the violence unleashed against them, was murdered with his companions on his way to say Mass. Romero is said to have spent hours in prayer beside the body. It was a turning point in his life – a kind of Damascus Road experience.

He excommunicated those responsible for the murders and set up a commission to monitor breaches of human rights. He began his famous sermons. Sunday after Sunday people packed the cathedral to hear of human rights violations during the previous week. He had plenty to report: murders of civilians (many of them peasants) and priests, intimidation of priests and catechists and much more.

He and his fellow bishop Rivera Damas issued a pastoral in which they condemned the 'institutional violence' directed against the 'poor majority' and appealed for a social consensus on their behalf. Most El Salvadorean bishops thought him unwise in his stance and influenced by an undesirable form of liberation theology. In another pastoral he dealt with three 'idolatries': worship of wealth, of private property and of political power.

In 1968 the Bishops' Conference of Latin America at their meeting in Medellin in Colombia, influenced by Pope Paul VI in his encyclical *Progress of Peoples* and by Archbishop Helder Camara of Recife in Brazil, had come out strongly in support of the oppressed poor in their countries. At the Conference meeting in Pueblo in Mexico, Romero with many others urged the bishops to maintain the Medellin line, which they did.

Recognition for him came from abroad in the Swedish Peace Prize for Ecumenical Action, in the nomination for the Nobel Peace Prize and in the honorary doctorate from the Catholic University of Louvain.

In 1979 a *junta*, supported by the United States, toppled the ruling president. The new mainly civilian government made some effort at reform. Left-wing elements rejected its programme as superficial and inadequate. Right-wing elements, including the 'Fourteen Families', were alarmed at plans to re-distribute land. Romero strongly felt that the government was not in control and was even a party to violence.

In an open letter of 17 February 1980 to President Carter of the United States, he said that the military were in political control and were oppressing the people on behalf of the El Salvadorean oligarchy and he appealed to him not to send military aid to El Salvador. On Sunday, 23 March in a sermon in the Sacred Heart Basilica he appealed directly to soldiers to obey their conscience rather than an immoral command.

It was surely these two appeals that forced his enemies to act swiftly. The day after the sermon he was celebrating Mass in the chapel of the hospital where he lived. Half way through the Mass four men entered the chapel. One of them fired with deadly accuracy.

> *Bishop's hands on strong dark head*
> *longed for ordination hour*
> *touch the chalice, touch the bread*
> *signs of sacramental power*
>
> *Rutilio amigo! friend of the poor*
> *wounded body, dead-cold hand*
> *pray for grace to work, endure*
> *for peace and justice in this land*
>
> *Word of God and wine and bread*
> *elements awaiting Christ*
> *only half a Mass is said*
> *another priest is sacrificed.*

Jean Donovan, lay missionary and ex-student of University College Cork, arrived in El Salvador in 1979. Dorothy Kazel, an Ursuline sister, had arrived about five years previous. Ita Forde and Maura Clarke, Maryknoll sisters, were assigned to El Salvador in 1980. All four women were working among the poor and were committed to obtaining justice for them. They were United States citizens and friends of Robert White, the United States ambassador, who shared their concerns.

On 2 December 1980, as they were travelling from San Salvador airport to the city, they were abducted by military personnel, brought to an off-road place and murdered. At least two of them were raped. It is likely that they were killed to intimidate missionaries who were witnesses to the crimes of the military against their own people. These brave women knew that they were living dangerously. The manner of their death probably came as no great surprise to them.

In the small hours of 16 November 1989 a detachment of soldiers broke into the Jesuit community house at the University of Central America in San Salvador. They first killed the elderly Joaquin Lopez y Lopez, director of a network of schools for the poor. They shot the other five (all members of the university staff) in the garden: Ignacio Ellacuria, rector of the University, and Amando Lopez (both of whom had done some of their religious formation in Dublin), Martin Baro, Segundo Montes and Juan Ramon Moreno.

The attack came after radio threats against Church personnel, including the University Jesuits who were seen as subversives because of their commitment to justice as well as to faith. Also murdered to eliminate witnesses were Elba Julia Ramos and her sixteen-year-old daughter Celina. They had taken refuge with the Jesuits after their house had been damaged by bombing or gunfire two days before.

Obdulio Ramos planted roses in the garden in memory of his wife and daughter and Jesuit friends. Another memorial to the University Eight is in the grounds of Milltown Park, Dublin, where Amando Lopez studied, prayed and was ordained.

Cattle graze where these four died
united with their crucified
Lord and people. Roses shine
where these eight drank bitter wine
of hate and greed. So life's not gone
beasts and grass and flowers live on
and four and eight make twelve in Christ
sealed, delivered, sacrificed
living witnesses with Him
that death and evil shall not win.

IN DUBLIN'S FAIR CITY

TOM KELLEHER, JOHN MCGUINNESS AND TOM DOYLE

Tom Kelleher

'Mrs O'Byrne,' the small dapper man said to his neighbour outside the church on 16 October 1982, 'you look lovely today. Just imagine how you will look in heaven.' That delightful blend of gallantry and faith was among the last words of Tom Kelleher. That evening he suffered a massive stroke. He went into a coma and died about two months later.

He was born on 16 June 1905 and christened Thomas Christopher on 19 June in the Church of Saint Nicholas of Myra in Francis Street, Dublin. He grew up in Golden Lane between Saint Patrick's Cathedral and Whitefriars Street Church – between Church of Ireland canons and Catholic Carmelites, one could say. Like many thousands of Dubliners at that time, the Kellehers were very poor and very Catholic.

Tom had his share of material hardship in his own adult life. He moved from job to job and at times he was unemployed. For a period he was away from his wife and family while he worked in Scotland. He gave his wages to his wife. They never had much money but they managed well with what they had. He delighted his children (and later his grandchildren) with his drawings and storytelling; he was quite a *'seanchaí'*, perhaps a gift from his Irish-speaking County Clare paternal ancestry.

He always had the faith but when he was a young married man he 'woke up' to what being a Catholic really meant: that it involved a personal following of Christ, a vocation to holiness. The 'awakening' came through a retreat or sermon which he attended. An important factor was a book or booklet given him by his mother-in-law. It seems to have been a work on the Blessed Sacrament, perhaps *The Imitation of Christ*, the fourth section of which is all about that tremendous fact of the faith.

The Eucharist became absolutely central to him. He was especially devoted to the Holy Name; he would murmur a word of reverence when he heard it misused. Another expression of his love for the Lord was his Pioneer pledge – it seems that the motive of reparation strongly appealed to him. He came to think of his day of baptism as his 'real' birthday and would celebrate it every 19 June by attending Mass in Francis Street Church, kneeling near the baptismal font and renewing his baptismal promises.

He kept a diary. Much of it is prayer, especially prayer for humility. It reveals that he had a strong sense of the presence of God in himself and in others. Evident in his writings is the fruit of his devotion to the Lord and of what came to characterise so much of his life: his extraordinary outreach to people. He was sociable, well-mannered and good-humoured; natural talents no doubt but enriched by grace. There was an impression of freedom and joy, something quite 'Franciscan'. It is no wonder he was attracted to the Third Order of the Saint of Assisi.

He had a strong sense of justice and once lost his job in a non-union firm when he approached the boss for a better wage for himself and his workmates. He was interested in the social teaching of the Church and became a student at the Jesuit-run Catholic Workers' College. He liked to express himself in words both spoken (he was a great talker) and written (he was a great letter writer in good causes and his handwriting was a work of art).

His most important apostolate was probably his work for youth in support of a local priest and kindred spirit, Father Larry Redmond. He was a 'leader' in the Don Bosco Youth Club, Drimnagh, run by the Sodality of Our Lady and linked with the Salesians. He helped many young men to lead good Christian lives and several of them became priests.

At one workplace he collected packed lunches from those work mates who did not want them and brought them to poor local children. He helped the poor with his social welfare money, leaving something in a local shop as payment for goods for those in need.

A formidable player in his young days, he boosted the morale of some not so good young footballers by organising a special 'roads league'. When he was porter in Crumlin Children's Hospital, his last job, he entertained the patients by reading stories to them (including 'stage effects'), especially to those from the country who had few visitors.

While he was terminally ill, his wife (who was to die not long after him) said that she did not begrudge him dying: 'He longed to see the face of God'. The date of his death seemed to betoken God's seal on his life: 26 December 1982. A special devotion of his was to the Holy Family. He would give couples with children he knew a Holy Family prayer card, telling them: 'Say that prayer to keep your marriage together'. Ordinarily in the Church calendar, 26 December is Saint Stephen's Day. In 1982 it fell on a Sunday and so it was the Feast of the Holy Family.

> *Families and children – yes, indeed*
> *others' children, then his own arrive*
> *their children too: for all a father's care*
> *all love, solicitude, no threat, no rod*
> *free lunch in Inchicore for those in need*
> *the youth are formed to be in Christ alive*
> *the sick get stories, B-teams get their share*
> *– he images the fatherhood of God.*

> *He celebrates in life, so too in death*
> *a Family that lived in Nazareth.*

John McGuinness

In 1924 a Dublin civil servant in the revenue department was organising a weekend retreat for his conference of the Society of Saint Vincent de Paul and their friends. One of those on his list cancelled at the last minute, so the organiser asked a colleague of his, a young Dubliner who had joined the permanent staff in 1920, to fill the gap. After some good-humoured resistance he said he would go if he could manage it, which he did. That weekend was to initiate a new life for him. The retreat-giver appealed for recruits to the Society and two weeks later, on 18 February 1924, the young man wrote his name in the roll-book: John Anthony McGuinness.

In the Dublin of his time the very poor comprised much of the population, but coming from a comfortable middle-class background, John had not been very conscious of them. But now he developed an extraordinary devotion to them. He was not ashamed to beg for them in cash and kind. Though a bachelor, he had an understanding of children and every winter barefoot children were his special care.

As well as visiting the poor in their homes, he met sailors in the Seamen's Institute and destitute men in the Vincent de Paul Night Shelter and helped to run an unemployed men's club. Activities included flag days, carol singing, raffles and pilgrimages. He paid the poor the compliment of being poor himself. Spending on himself was reduced to a minimum and the bulk of his income went to Church missions and the poor. Recreation (including golf – he swung a formidable club) was cut down or cut out, with the possible exception of swimming. Holidays were spent in or near Dublin so as not to interfere with his charity work and presumably for the same reason he moved into a modest city flat.

The disciplined and austere life and love of the poor were linked to daily Mass and Communion, to his membership of the Franciscan Third Order and to what amounted to semi-continuous prayer. The discipline was noted by his work colleagues. He had always been a conscientious worker but now a new 'work ethic' became evident. Did the revenue department have a saint on its hands?

The following account illustrates his one-to-one concern for those in need. He met a man who had lost faith in everything, including himself. Despite rebuffs John persevered with him. The man had poor eyesight but loved reading, so John got him a magnifying glass. The man had good 'mending' hands and so John brought him defective rosary beads, reminding him that he was helping others. Thus the man no longer felt unwanted. Finally, one Thursday they went to confession together and the next day they were together at Mass and Communion – the first of many Fridays of joint rendezvous with the Lord.

Nearly all of this pattern of commitment developed after the International Eucharistic Congress in 1932. That great event in the religious history of Dublin seems to have been for him a moment of profound and far-reaching dedication.

He drove himself hard – too hard for health. The severe winter of 1946–1947 did not help. A doctor pronounced him badly run-down and under-nourished. His efforts and plans to recoup his health came too late. He died on 14 February 1947, shortly after the twenty-third anniversary of the momentous 'fill the gap' retreat.

This Dublin glory of the Saint Vincent de Paul Society and the Franciscan Third Order had often spoke of death as a going home. So, to those who loved him and knew him well, the beginnings of a smile on his face in death was no great surprise but rather a suggestion of a welcome and joy beyond words.

John serves the State, the people – yes, indeed
he serves God too, his people in their need
those whose lives the world considers loss
he sees them all anointed by the Cross
and so he listens, tries to understand
is there to pray and hope and hold the hand
thinking perhaps how John had heard the beat
of Christ's own Heart, seen wounded hands and feet.

Tom Doyle

'I was cycling along the North Strand, Dublin, with a friend, Michael Murphy, when the rain forced us to shelter under a railway bridge where a mutual acquaintance also took shelter. The latter informed us that he would have to go on to his Vincent de Paul meeting. This interested me and I arranged to go to the next meeting which was in Myra House'. So Tom Doyle described the event that led to his life of commitment to the poor.

He was born in Rathvilly, County Carlow, in 1905. His parents died when he was young and relatives took care of the children. After schooling by the Patrician Brothers in Carlow he came to Dublin to work. He joined the Society of Saint Vincent de Paul at Myra House in the south inner city, where the Legion of Mary had been founded in 1921. In 1927 the Legion opened the Morning Star hostel in the north inner city for homeless men. In 1929, after a visit to the hostel, Tom joined the Legion as a member of the praesidium (the basic working unit of the Legion) that staffed the Morning Star.

The hostel was an eye-opener and heart-mover for him. His sister-in-law recalled how one night he came out of deep thought and said suddenly: 'Our Lady has shown me the way I should go. I'm going to become an indoor brother of the hostel'. It was a very radical decision. Becoming an indoor brother meant making the hostel his home and full-time workplace. It entailed accepting a simple and regulated lifestyle and, in his case, giving up a good job, which not everyone had the luxury of at that time of economic depression.

When he became hostel manager in 1931, he had two elderly indoor brothers and one praesidium to help him to care for one hundred and fifty residents. He established another praesidium, which in turn 'mothered' others. (The great majority of hostel legionaries were 'outdoor' brothers who combined hostel service with other commitments and activities.)

He had a daily routine of two early Masses – which he served with Communion at the first of them – in the nearby Capuchin church, dormitory maintenance, helping with meals, cleaning, heating and so on. A favourite 'indulgence' of his was presiding at afternoon tea and a favourite priority was personal attention to the residents. He once said: 'There is a danger that we may fall short in our service by not giving full personal attention to each man. We should get to know them intimately, share their interests and as friends show an interest in their hopes and desires'.

There are reports of the fruits of his personal one-to-one attention both face-to-face and through correspondence: the hostel 'heart scald' who after years without the sacraments was a daily communicant in his last months of life; the alcoholic ex-army officer and university graduate who started a new life and with his wife came into the Church; and the ex-residents in prison who asked him to visit them, including the one he visited on the eve of his execution and who said of a newly arrived statue of Our Lady at the hostel, 'I'll be looking down in heaven on it tomorrow'.

He had a patient and peaceable temperament that encouraged 'problem people' and helped him to cope with difficult and, on occasion, violent situations. He was Tom the tranquil.

A special service he provided was a discussion group every so often on matters of faith or associated with faith. This developed into the 'Patricians', now a major Legion apostolate.

A very joyful event was the granting of reservation of the Blessed Sacrament to the hostel. Tom moved to a room near the chapel to be a protection against any possible irreverence by a disturbed resident and also, no doubt, for his own devotion. The chapel, with its appropriately star-shaped sanctuary lamp and some of its décor the work of a hostel brother and a hostel resident, was a haven of prayer for himself and many others.

His apostolic interests extended beyond the Morning Star. He helped the work of the Legion in the nearby Regina Coeli Hostel for women and children. He went on Legion work to Britain, Sweden and other parts of Ireland and he was contact officer between Legion headquarters and India. He did a stint as vice- president of the Legion. He spent his last years in a retirement full of Mass, prayer, reading and quiet apostolate. He died on 30 October 1992. In keeping with his wish, his remains rest with those of his beloved poor in the Morning Star plot in Glasnevin cemetery.

> *Tom serves God's people: She the Morning Star*
> *guides them to his door from near and far*
> *he sees her Son in them, her face and His*
> *believes the gospel and all its promises*
> *and so he listens, tries to understand*
> *is there to pray and hope and hold the hand*
> *thinking perhaps how Thomas found his way*
> *from Christ in death to Christ on Easter Day.*

SWEET PRINCE

BAUDOUIN OF THE BELGIANS

The driver of the car was passing a village shrine of Our Lady when he noticed that some mocker had put a First World War German helmet on the head of the statue. He stopped the car, got out, went over to the shrine, whipped off the helmet, returned to the car and drove on. Not a word was spoken during the whole episode. Baudouin of the Belgians was not going to tolerate an insult to his Mother.

He was born on 7 September 1930, the son of Leopold, heir to the Belgian throne, and the beautiful Astrid of Sweden, and grandson of Albert, the great hero-king of the First World War. On the death of Albert in 1934, his father became Leopold III. The following year Astrid was killed in a car crash in Switzerland.

On 10 May 1940, the Germans invaded Belgium. Leopold led a brave resistance, but with his troops encircled he surrendered and became a prisoner among his people. His government felt that he should have joined them in exile in London. The British and French regarded his surrender as a betrayal of them. In 1944, with the Allied invasion of Europe, Leopold, with his entire family (children both of Astrid and of his second wife, Princess de Réthy), were deported to Germany and then to Austria. They were in Switzerland for some years while post-war Belgium debated Leopold's position. This 'crisis of the Crown' ended in 1951 when Leopold formally abdicated and Baudouin was proclaimed king.

He tried to insulate the monarchy from the political turmoil and to make it a centre of unity for his regionalised and ethnically-divided kingdom, and a healing influence after the trauma surrounding his father. In this he was helped by a deep religious faith, which went back to his teenage 'discovery' of Jesus' personal love for him and his presence in him and in others.

In his first few years as king he gave the impression of being serious and withdrawn, but the ebullient African-style welcome he received in the then Belgian Congo in 1955 evoked a more rapportive Baudouin, and this new persona happily proved permanent. Then it was time to think of marriage.

The future Cardinal Suenens put him in touch with the remarkable Veronica O'Brien of the Legion of Mary. She became his spiritual guide and undertook to find a spouse for him among the Spanish aristocracy. She found the deeply religious Fabiola de Mora y Aragon. The devout and delightful drama ended in Lourdes in July 1960 when after Mass and a long walk Fabiola accepted his proposal. They were married five months later. Both of them believed that Our Lady had a hand in their romance; in his journal, Baudouin wrote of 'her new miracle' and Fabiola wrote to Veronica O'Brien, 'I never knew that Our Lady was a match-maker'.

They were very much in love and showed it. A king and queen who walked hand in hand in public was a godsend to the popular press and a delight and an example to the nation. In his journal, he is prayerfully ecstatic about his wife, but to their sorrow all her pregnancies ended in miscarriages. They saw that this suffering meant, as he told some guests, 'that our heart was freer to love all children, absolutely all children.' Indeed, as the journal records, there was a shared reach-out spirituality behind all the receptions, visits, speeches, handshakes and smiles. This royal pair embodied royal prayer.

He went to Mass every day and there was a daily period of prayer, usually in the morning. The journal reveals a humble man to whom intimacy with Jesus and Mary was very important. Perhaps his attentiveness to the Lord and his Mother had something to do with his gift of listening to others and of slipping 'the word of faith' into conversation at an opportune moment. An assessment of him as sovereign called him 'the embodiment of the national conscience'.

Conscience made itself felt with special urgency in 1989 when a bill to legalise abortion was in process in parliament. To sign or not to sign? He told Fabiola that refusal to sign might entail renouncing the throne, but in the event it did not come to that. He invoked an 'unable to govern' clause in the constitution that allowed the suspension of his sovereignty for one day while the government/parliament enacted the bill. He said that he could not sign into law a bill that contravened his religious beliefs. 'The Pope himself,' he told his ministers, 'would not make me change my mind.'

His last years were marked by heart attacks and he died on 31 July 1993. At Fabiola's request, his internationally televised funeral was a celebration of thanksgiving and hope. The Cardinal Archbishop of Brussels-Malines preached an eloquent sermon, but the real sermon was Fabiola's: she wore white.

Happy the people with a king like this
he kept his word, his promises
a 'Joseph', straight and just
a man you'd trust

He loved his people, made his life for them
a kind of prayer, a great Amen
of power and innocence
Goodnight, sweet prince.

DEFENDER OF THE LITTLE ONES

JEROME LEJEUNE

Something very unusual happened at a major sporting event for the intellectually handicapped. Two sprinters, both of them with Down Syndrome, raced side by side. One of them forged ahead, then stumbled and fell. His companion stopped, lifted him up, massaged his knees and embraced him. Together they shared podium honours and emotion swept the stands. Spectators had been given a lesson in love.

Down Syndrome participants focused on one spectator. They embraced him and emblazoned him with their golds, silvers and bronzes. He was the man who had defended their dignity, given them a new name and identity and discredited 'mongolism' and 'Down Syndrome' with their prejudiced connections. The former term came from the belief that their physical appearance denoted a link with the inhabitants of Mongolia. The latter term commemorated the mid-nineteenth century Sir Langdon Down, apparently a believer in white racial superiority, who described the handicap as 'Mongolian idiocy'.

This spectator was Jerome Lejeune. He was born in 1926 in Montrouge, south-west of Paris. He graduated in medicine at the University of Paris and his hospital experience gave him a compassionate interest in children affected with Down Syndrome. He noted both their 'head' (the somewhat limited intelligence, especially in abstract subjects) and their 'heart' (their often affectionate nature) and wondered what role genetics had to play in the matter. Thus he began his meticulous research.

Assisted by Raymond Turpin and Marthe Gauthier, he focused on chromosomes, the rod-like cell carriers of genes, arranged in side-by-side pairs. In 1956 Tjio and Leven had established that in an average human being each cell had twenty-three pairs, i.e. forty-six chromosomes. In 1959 the Paris Three announced the discovery in Down Syndrome children of a forty-seventh chromosome, physically identical with the twenty-first pair.

This seminal discovery of 'trisomie twenty-one', as he called it, gave new impetus to genetics research and made the traditional names with their prejudiced nuance obsolete. It also gave him a doctorate and an international reputation. He never discovered a way of preventing the trisomic condition but he did develop treatments that improved intelligence and activity.

In Paris he ran a free consultancy (even after it lost state funding) and became a legend of one-to-one compassion and respect for human dignity to parents and children who came there from various countries. Genetics brought him to Russia, Israel, Chile and Japan. (He was much taken by the Japanese word for womb, *shikyuu*, with a literal meaning of 'infant's temple'). He worked in the United States where he was a member of the American Academy of Arts and Sciences (receiving the Kennedy Prize from JFK himself) and with a United Nations committee of congenital abnormalities. Pope Paul VI made him a member of the Pontifical Academy of Sciences and he was elected to the French Academy of Moral and Political Sciences.

Along with all this he led a family life that was deeply and openly Christian. He was married to the Danish Birthe Bringsted who shared his values and interests. They had five children. This pattern of family faith and fulfilment must surely have helped him in the war he waged during his later years: the defence of unborn human life.

He realised that the famous chromosome discovery could be misused for the aborting of trisomic babies. This danger and his mission to confront it came poignantly home to him when a tearful trisomic youngster flung himself into his arms and begged him to defend those like him still unborn. He told his genetics team that he was determined to fight for his trisomic 'sick' awaiting birth.

He became a brilliant defender of human life on platforms, television and radio, but too brilliant for some; after one telecast his wife heard a studio executive say to a producer: 'Lejeune? That pig! But what talent! He's too good. Don't invite him again.' He and his friends had to cope with an array of anti-life activism, some of it mindless and menacing.

What immensely saddened him was the abandonment by so many doctors of their pro-life oath-bound Hippocratic ethos. At an international medical conference on health in New York, which was favouring the legalising of abortion, he did not mince his words: 'This Institute of Health is an Institute of Death'. That evening he wrote to his wife: 'This afternoon I lost my Nobel Prize'.

He was the leading light in the establishing of the World Federation of Doctors who Respect Human life (from conception to death), chairperson of Laissez-le Vivres and president of the Society for the Protection of Unborn Children. He set up 'The Houses of Tom Thumb' for mothers tempted to abort because of materially difficult situations.

He was an adviser and informant of Pope John Paul II on genetics and related issues. They became real friends and to the Pope he was 'Brother Jerome'. He and his wife lunched with John Paul only hours before the assassination attempt on 13 May 1981. It is very likely that he influenced the text of *The Gospel of Life*, perhaps John Paul's greatest encyclical. Here and there in the section on abortion the Pope's very strong words seem to echo Lejeune's in his pro-life crusade – an expression perhaps of the convergence of mind and heart that united them in friendship.

In 1994 John Paul made him the first president of the Pontifical Academy of Life. The Pope knew that Lejeune was dying of cancer and the appointment was a farewell accolade from one great Christian humanist to another. He was president for thirty-three days. His 'little ones' were in his mind to the end.

He died on Easter Sunday, 3 April 1994. Many, including the Pope, saw a 'sign' in that this great apostle of life departed on the great feast-day of the Lord of Life. Notre Dame de Paris was packed for the funeral Mass. The officiating bishop read John Paul's message in which the Pope thanked God for 'Brother Jerome' and praised him for all that he had done for human life and dignity, and for his brave and challenging witness to a permissive society.

But the speaker who impressed most was the trisomic Bruno, who had been one of the children involved in the famous discovery of thirty-five years previous. He spoke of and to Lejeune from his heart: 'Thank you, Professor Lejeune, for all that you have done for my father and my mother. Thanks to you, I am proud to be me. Your death has healed me'. Bruno was only one of many who were proud to be themselves because of Jerome Lejeune. This man of faith and science had been the protecting and leading father of a very large family; in this he was a disciple of the Lord of little ones who made them in their innocence and trustfulness role-models of the Christian life.

Lejeune, the young one, so well named
called to protect the very young
newly arrived, on the lowest rung
of the ladder of life and under threat
because they're ill – but don't forget
they are of us. So he proclaimed
in science and faith, in deed and word:
'A human's here, a tiny 'who'
a miracle completely new
a wonder-gift, an infant given
meant like all of us for heaven
a little one loved by the Lord'.

Easter Day, all labour done
rendezvous with Mary's Son
once a very little one
now the Lord of life, says 'Come'.

BY DODDER AND MOY

TEDDY BYRNE, KEVIN MCDOWELL, PADDY WATSON, VINCENT SMYTH AND YVONNE (AQUINAS) MCNULTY

Teddy Byrne, Kevin McDowell and Paddy Watson

Teddy Byrne was a special friend of my youth. He lived at 62 Home Villas, Donnybrook, Dublin, not far from the river Dodder. He was an only son, the adored hope and joy of his parents, two sisters and aunt. I associate that house not only with the Byrnes but with two pieces of music, still favourites of mine, which I heard there: the wonderful opening theme of Mozart's Fortieth Symphony and 'It's Raining Sunbeams', sung by the movie star Deanna Durbin – Teddy and I were ardent fans of hers. In their tunefulness and rhythm the pieces were in some way the musical counterparts of his cheerful temperament and a lifestyle that was disciplined without being harsh.

He was of low and sturdy build with freckled face and deft movements – the last point meaning in his case that he was good at football and tennis. We played tennis together, mostly at Belfield, the newly acquired property of University College Dublin. He nearly always won.

This young man of an almost radiant innocence and goodness had his heart set on being a priest. He was or had been a Mass-server in his parish church; it may well have been at the altar that the thought had first come to him.

Two Donnybrook friends of his and mine also had the priesthood in mind: the stalwart and soft-spoken northerner, Kevin McDowell (formidable at football, I recall), who was to have a long ministry divided between the Archdiocese of Dublin and the Society of Jesus; and the gentle and delicate Paddy Watson, also of Home Villas, who died young on the threshold, as it were, of his preparation for the priesthood.

An Australian bishop accepted Teddy for his diocese, so on leaving Synge Street Christian Brothers' secondary school he entered All Hallows College, Dublin. I left the same school for

UCD and after three years there went in 1940 to the Jesuit novitiate.

I remember that summer evening in 1941 when I returned from a walk to be told of his death. Then or later I learned that he had haemorrhaged and collapsed just at the start of a football match in All Hallows. Not long before his death he had said that he would prefer to die 'now' when he felt full of love for God, rather than to die hardened and less loving later in life. Did he have a premonition?

Father Purcell, the spiritual director of the All Hallows students, wrote to me to say that Teddy was 'special', an outstanding seminarian, and that he was thinking of writing something about him. He asked if I had any letters of his, but I didn't; his letters were about ordinary things and I had not kept them. I still remember his microscopic handwriting.

The idea came to me around the time of my ordination of making my life as a priest as a 'doubling up' of the ministry he never had. I see now that it was too ambitious an aspiration. I think of him when I am in Belfield or Donnybrook and I occasionally visit his grave in All Hallows. He is certainly in what I call my mini-communion of saints.

The Latin inscription on his gravestone asks for prayers for Edward Joseph Byrne, who died on 22 May 1941 aged twenty-one and quotes psalm 131/132: 'This is my resting place which I have chosen'. The text, to the best of my recollection, was selected by Father Purcell because of Teddy's above-mentioned pre-death remark. It sums up his life: he had chosen God and God, in a way beyond our ordinary understanding, had chosen him.

Vincent Smyth

Maureen Conmee had a sudden intuition about a young man she was coaching in Irish for the Leaving Certificate and decided to voice it there and then: 'Vincent, I think you have a vocation to be a priest'. He reddened from ear to ear: 'I've been thinking about that for five years and you guess it in a minute!'

Vincent Smyth was born in Ballina on the Moy in County Mayo on 16 May 1965, the third youngest in the family. He enrolled in the Mercy Junior Boys' School at the time that Sister Aquinas, or otherwise known as Yvonne McNulty, was principal there. Nearly all his secondary schooling was at Saint Muredach's College. For his Leaving Certificate he went to school in Foxford and to Maureen Conmee for special tuition in Irish.

She recalls how they would chat over a cup of tea, how on a rainy night she would lend him a raincoat that he would return washed and she noted his wit and his joyful outlook on life. One memory is very special: his remark about dying in a hurry and having a concelebrated funeral Mass. Was it just a joke or was it a premonition?

This young man did a power of good in his milieu. He befriended a girl in school who was shunned by others and he brought a few friends who had become religiously careless back to Mass attendance. As a voluntary worker in Saint Joseph's hospital he laid out the dead (an unusual task for a teenager) with total ease: 'This did not bother him in the least', remarked Maureen Conmee.

He was a member of the Western Care Association and of the Legion of Mary and said the rosary with the residents of the Western Care House. He was president of the local junior branch of the Saint Joseph's Young Priests' Society and it may well have been his Saint Joseph's work that gave him his dream of becoming a priest.

Where to go to realise the dream? He finally decided on the Salesians, no doubt because of their apostolate to young people. The Salesian who interviewed him was impressed. He could look forward to joining them after the Leaving Certificate.

He died of a heart attack on 28 January 1984. His funeral with concelebrated Mass was on 31 January, the feast day of Saint John Bosco, founder of the Order he planned to join. He had indeed died in a hurry. Perhaps God was in a hurry too.

Yvonne (Aquinas) McNulty
I remember joking with Sister Aquinas/Yvonne McNulty: 'When you're beatified or canonised, the official portrait will show you stepping from one car into another'. She was certainly a woman of journeys in the latter part of her life, first nationally, then internationally; planes replacing cars, as it were.

Her first major journey was across Ireland from Dublin to Ballina to become a Sister of Mercy, leaving behind a much shaken and disapproving father. A Protestant, he had kept his promise at marriage to allow his children to be reared Catholics, but a daughter becoming a nun, and so faraway too, was something else. He was not the last to experience the McNulty determination. He was to die a Catholic, no doubt largely because of her very determined prayers.

The life she was committing herself to was vow-based, with lots of prayer and work and (in those pre-Vatican II days) lots of rules and regulations. Her creative mind must have often wrestled with that last-mentioned item.

The main work was teaching. She was engaged in school work for many years in both Belmullet, where she helped to found a secondary school, and in Ballina, where her service included being principal of the Junior Boys' School from 1962 to 1975. She retired from teaching in 1979.

However, she began a new career. New horizons had begun to beckon. She began her 'second journey' (this one of the mind and heart), taking a new direction, following a new vocation in her life. In this she had distinguished forerunners in Christian history: Paul, Augustine, Thomas Becket, Ignatius Loyola, Camillus de Lellis, Vincent de Paul, John Henry Newman, Matt Talbot, Edith Stein and C.S. Lewis.

Her journey began in Ballina with helping to found a community centre and hostels for wheelchair invalids, which led to a local landmark achievement: Emmanuel House. All this entailed much journeying, haunting of officialdom, a hands-on approach, animating others and nitty-gritty detail. The determination was flavoured with a certain lightheartedness, and behind and in it all much prayer.

Having seen Emmanuel established and under Cheshire and local committee care, she turned to confront a new horror and to serve a new category of people in need: AIDS and AIDS sufferers. She went to Galway to help AIDS patients and then to Boston for practical training in AIDS nursing. She travelled across Europe to Romania to care for orphans in substandard living conditions, many of them HIV-infected. The Romanian experience must have been the most harrowing of her life. It must have tested her courage, of which she had plenty, to an extreme. 'Courage,' she used to say, 'is doing what you are afraid to do.'

After Romania she returned to Ballina and on to Brazil: from Danube to Moy to Amazon. Compared to Romania it must have felt like paradise. She was a member of a Killala diocesan mission in the diocese of Miracema. She was at home with Killala clergy and laity and had good rapport with the local people. Now closing in on eighty years old and not in the best of health, she knew that her time was short and spoke of burial in Brazil. She died suddenly on 29 January 1997 at Colinas. The simple memorial marking her grave has a text in Portuguese from the Acts of the Apostles with only the pronoun changed: 'She went about doing good'. That says it all.

Dodder in Dublin, Moy in Mayo – flow on
these crossed your bridges, walked on your banks:
Teddy, Paddy, Kevin, Vincent, Yvonne
these we remember, for these we give thanks.

They were like rivers – three of them short, two long
pure and life-giving, no base alloy
flowing in freedom, singing a hope-filled song
into the ocean of God's own joy.

SOURCES

The main source for 'The Rock' and 'The Light on the Road' was the New Testament, with texts taken from the New Revised Standard Version of the Holy Bible. The Catholic Encyclopaedia (1967 edition) was helpful, especially for 'Wheat and Bread', 'Witnesses in Word', 'White Martyrs', 'Medieval Mosaic', 'Across the Sea', 'American Cameos', 'Words and Music' and for data concerning the Venerable John Travers in Vol. 7, p. 640 and Vol. 9, p. 323.

Special thanks to the Kelleher family for sharing their memories of their father; to Fr Michael O'Sullivan SJ for material on the companions of Oscar Romero; to the Sisters of Mercy, Ballina, Anthony Hughes and Cyril Hynes for material on Sister Aquinas (Yvonne) McNulty, John A. McGuinness and Tom Doyle respectively; to Maureen Conmee for information on Vincent Smyth and to Celia Smyth for permission to re-publish an article on her son.

Alzin, Josse, *A Dangerous Little Friar*, Dublin: Clonmore and Reynolds, 1957.

Anon., *John A. McGuinness, Friend of the Poor*, Dublin: Irish Messenger Office, imprimatur 1948.

Bede, *The Ecclesiastical History of the English People* (eighth century).

Brodrick SJ, James, *Saint Francis Xavier*, London, Burns and Oates, 1952

Brodrick SJ, James, *A Procession of Saints*, London: Burns and Oates, 1949.

Burgess, Alan, *The Small Woman*, New York: Evans Brothers, 1971.

Burke-Savage SJ, Roland, *A Valiant Dublin Woman*, Dublin: M.H. Gill, 1940.

Casey, Michael (ed.), *The Frédéric Ozanam Story*, Dublin: SVP Publications, Ireland, 1976.

Catholic, Anglican and Pioneer Records, *Janani Luwum and Companions*. Chambers, R.W., *Thomas More*, London: Jonathan Cape, 1935.

Chesterton, G.K., *Autobiography*, London: Hutchinson, 1936.

Claude, Robert, *The Soul of Pier-Giorgio Frassati*, translated by Una Morrissey, Cork: Mercier, 1960.

Clear SJ, John B., *Elizabeth of Hungary: Princess, Wife, Mother, Saint*, Dublin: Irish Messenger Office, 1985.

Curtayne, Alice, *Saint Catherine of Siena*, London: Sheed and Ward, 1929.

Dov SJ, John, *Strange Vagabond of God*, Dublin: Ward River Press, 1983.

Forest, Jim, *Love is the Measure*, New York: Paulist Press, 1986.

Hebbelthwaite, Peter, *John XXIII*, London: Geoffrey Chapman, 1985.

Keogh, Dermot, *Romero, El Salvador's Martyr*, Dublin: Dominican Publications, 1981.

Legion of Mary Archives, *Alfie Lambe*.

Legion of Mary Archives, *Tom Doyle*.

Lejuene-Gaymard, Clara, *La Vie est un Bonheur*, Paris: Criterion, 1997.

Lewis, C.S., *Surprised by Joy*, London: G. Bles, 1955.

Martindale SJ, C.C., *Life of Saint Camillus*, London: Sheed and Ward, 1949.

McGrath SJ, Fergal, *Father John Sullivan SJ*, London: Longmans, 1941.

Millett, OFM, Benignus, et al, *Archbishop O'Hurley and Companions*, Rome: Congregation for Causes of Saints and Diocese of Dublin, 1988.

SOURCES

Norman, Mrs George, *The Life and Martyrdom of Father Michael Pro, SJ*, London: Catholic Book Club, 1938 (reprint).

O'Farrell PBVM, Mary Pius, *Woman of the Gospel*, Cork and Monasterevin: Cork Publishing Ltd. for Generalate of Sisters of the Presentation of the Blessed Virgin Mary, 1996.

Perpetua, Saturus and Tertullian, *The Passion of Perpetua and Felicity* (third century).

Purcell, Mary, *Matt Talbot and his Times*, Dublin: M.H. Gill, 1955.

Suenens, Leon-Joseph, *Edel Quinn*, Dublin: Fallon, 1954.

Suenens, Leon-Joseph, *Baudouin, King of the Belgians*, translated by Helen M. Synne SIJ, Ertvelde: F.A.A.T. Publications, 1996.

Teresa of the Holy Spirit, *Edith Stein*, translated by Cecily Hastings and Donald Nicholl, London: Sheed and Ward, 1952.

Thérèse of Lisieux, *Autobiography of a Saint*, translated by Ronald Knox, London: Collins (Fontana), 1960.

Zahn, Gordon C., *In Solitary Witness*, Collegeville: The Liturgical Press, 1964.